God Spoke And He Sounded Like....

To my dear neighbors Chris & Magan

God Bless

Norman
July 19, 2007

Copyright © 2006 Norman Taylor
All rights reserved.
ISBN: 1-4196-2913-1

To order additional copies, please contact us.
BookSurge, LLC
www.booksurge.com
1-866-308-6235
orders@booksurge.com

NORMAN TAYLOR

GOD SPOKE AND HE SOUNDED LIKE....

A Book Of Christian Testimonials

2006

God Spoke And He Sounded Like....

TABLE OF CONTENTS

Introduction	xiii
The Invitation	1
Time Changer	5
Mere Brokenness…Enough?	9
Mac	11
Missionaries and Mentors	15
"Luke"	17
Jesus the Manager	21
Ecuador	27
Carl Brown	37
Alex	43
A. J. Hewett	47
Credere	55
Media Naranja	61
Whitney	69
Kelly	73
South Carolina	79
Anyway	85
"The Real Norman Taylor"	87
Phil Washer	95
The Long Ten Feet	97
Charlie Missroon	103
Mary Duncan, Mother	107
Hearts for Heaven	111
Taxi Robert	119

Kevin	123
Disney Dads	129
The "Wisdom" of the Comic Strips	131
Robert L. Williams and Miracle Making Ministries	133
Stones	141
Jim and Bobby	149
The Seamstress	155
"Let's help out a little sister..."	161
"I didn't pray again last night, Reb"	179
The Offering Takers	183
Reba Sims, Den Mother	187
Conclusion	193
Appendix: A Christians Hierarchy of Needs	195
Bibliography	199

For Bret, Who Never Let Me Give Up

For My Wife Margaret, For Her Love And Support

For Kelly And Whitney, My Beloved Daughters

INTRODUCTION

Bound in these pages are stories of some seemingly ordinary people, a diverse group: retired widows, El Salvadoran taxi drivers, business managers, Ecuadorian lay ministers, stationery salesmen, children (tons of them), and so on. But something makes these people really very extraordinary. That "something" lies in the way they made, and continue to make, differences in other people's lives (like mine) through their witness.

The original working title of this book was "Lessons I Learned the Hard Way That You Can Have for $19.95." At the beginning of the writing process, that pretty much described my feelings about a life of mis-steps and errors. Along the way, at all the right times, God put one of these "ordinary people" in my path to teach me a very valuable lesson or rekindle my faith. The purpose of this book is to share those lessons and to share God's glory as reflected in these human lives. After all, none of us can really teach anything all by ourselves, we can only properly make the example through the channels of our personal relationship with God.

As dedicated Christians seeking nourishment in the Word, we often wrestle with particular scriptures, digging for their meaning. We find lots of room for friendly disagreement. One such example: A recent discussion in our Sunday School class on the subject of "where heaven physically exists." Although many of the 57 people in attendance were extremely well versed scripturally, no two of them gave the same answer.

The thirst for a clear vision of God seems to be eternal in man. Consider that perhaps the earliest superstition is that of knocking on wood for good luck. The source of this myth involves a misguided reverence for trees; the belief that the pyrotechnics of lightning strikes is evidence of a powerful spirit residing in the timber. Men of ancient times apparently believed that lightning was God's way of communication with the plant, so they called upon the devastated wood to yield up his secrets. Imperfect as their vision was, they were still striving for something great: a personal relationship with God.

To many believers, this search for Truth is ceaselessly rewarding. Each new question is cause for immersion in the Word. For others, the process becomes a bit like the weekend duffer playing golf with God. Many Christians restlessly scour translations and study guides in search of verbiage that best suits their own concept of a verse, or a reconciliation of disturbing passages.1

However much we wrestle with the details of our Christian faith, we must accept that man can never entirely get his arms around God and his enigmas. To understand this, consider our inability to comprehend just one simple item in His vast inventory of mysteries: eternity. If we acknowledge that eternity is merely a concept of space and time, then how much more inadequate are we to understand his capacities for deeper concepts like love, mercy, grace, etc. As the well-worn but accurate saying goes, "He is God, and we are not."

Should our questioning, our differing views, and our recognition that we have incomplete vision make us feel inferior in faith, substandard as Christian believers? Should it cause unhealthy discord among us? Of course not. While certainly there are believers who are better grounded in the faith or more Biblically literate than other believers, we *all* fall *quite* short of the glory of God, as scripture tells us over and over.2 On a scale from one to ten, with Jesus at ten, we would none score higher than an infinitesimal fraction. This will always be true, no matter how profound we perceive the strength of our faith, the might of our works, or the wisdom of our interpretive powers to be. Nonetheless, this limitation should never deter us from continually working to live out God's Will for our lives. Imperfection should not beget a failure of the heart, mind or spirit.

One recent sermon from my pastor of the time, Dr John Bryan, commenced with these four letters projected on the sanctuary wall: "F. I. D. O." As I pondered some possible canine connection, he translated the acronym as "Forget It, Drive On." By that, he did not mean that we should forget our sinfulness or turn from the Bible. Rather, he meant that we should not let our imperfect visions and sinful natures prevent us from pressing on to do God's work.

To add the words of Charles L. Allen, (*my emphasis*) "The Christian is not one who has gone all the way with Christ. *None of us has.* The Christian is one who has found the right road." And, from The Allure of Hope by Jan Meyer: "God seems to be more concerned with our trust-that He is taking us somewhere because of his love for us, than He is concerned with a flawless record along the way."3

There is no intent here to trivialize the value of experiencing God's Word at a deeper level (that is, to be more Biblically literate). Rather, the idea is simply this: Before we aspire to higher Biblical scholarship, let's work on being a living example for and a true friend to the others in our lives. Having found God's grace through salvation, let us first dedicate our lives to the concept of witness by our works. Works follow faith, they are not its substitute, but necessarily for the Christian they must follow.4 And, let's hold to these fundamentals regardless of the depth of our Christian learning as we progress. The term "baby Christians" more accurately describes those who fail to practice these concepts than it does those who have incomplete Biblical knowledge. I have heard many believers say "I'm not as good a Christian as (that person) because I don't know the Bible as well as they do." In so doing, they were missing the value of using the other spiritual gifts in their toolbox.

A secular parallel might be found in Abraham Maslow's "hierarchy of needs." In Maslow's view, before a person can achieve higher levels of "being," he must first satisfy basic physical needs of sustenance: food, water, air, shelter. In the same sense, before we aspire to higher Biblical literacy, we must first grasp the spiritual fundamentals of salvation, faith, personal relationship with God, and good deeds.5 We should also recognize that the bottom levels of hierarchical triangles (see Appendix) are larger than the top levels for a reason: a great deal of foundation building is needed first.

This manuscript focuses on just one aspect of God's wonderful powers, albeit a major one: His ability to use humans to carry out his missions, to help us be "on the right road." Once, following a time of great personal depression, I was asked to give a talk on my recovery. I found myself saying "God spoke, and He sounded like Scott Torrence" (a friend who had helped me to recovery). Then I found myself repeating that phrase over and over, substituting different names, incorporating friend upon friend into the presentation, and mentioning specifically how God had worked through them on my behalf.

We often lament how it seems that God doesn't perform any miracles on earth any more, as He did in Old Testament times. No more Elijah dousing wood with water three times and yet God was still able to set it on fire,6 no more walls felled by mere trumpet blasts. In so doing, we totally miss the human miracles all around us. We miss the miracle of people in our lives reaching within themselves to perform totally selfless acts, exercising personal courage that to us might be thoroughly impossible, demonstrating love in ways we could not.

For the most part, this book is an assemblage of those works. It is a celebration of lives and acts guided by God's principles, salted with (indeed) offerings of lessons I learned the hard way that hopefully the reader may indeed obtain far more inexpensively. And, along the way, I finally learned enough to offer a few lessons of my own. At the end of each chapter, reference is made to scriptural passages which amplify the Biblical principles exercised by the subject, or contrast the subject to a Biblical character.

The focus here is on God's role as humanities' Divine Tillerman, in both senses of "tilling," as both our cultivator and guide. From this partial view of God's powers, we should also gain increased appreciation for all the other roles that He necessarily plays in the universe.

THE INVITATION

On my mantle at home, there is a small statue entitled, simply, "The Invitation." I bought it at the Lifeway Christian Store in Augusta, Georgia. I bought it "as is"; no box, no explanatory material, no brochure. In time, I learned to appreciate that this allowed me to interpret the sculpture in my own way, to see what God wanted me to see personally, from my personal relationship with Him. I see a little more every time I look at it.

There are two figures cast in plaster, Jesus and a man. Jesus stands firmly in the clear blue air; the man kneels on a section of white cloud. The man's suspension is made possible only by the fact that he is firmly grasping Jesus' hand. The Savior is clad in a white robe wrapped in a powder blue parabola of sash, his head covered by a matching hood. His face can only be seen clearly by looking at it from the man's humble perspective. It is not a portrayal of God's Son as young and handsome. The face is craggy, reflecting experience and wisdom far beyond a man of 30 or so earthly years. His eyebrows are thick, his chin angular. The man is clad in simple modern garb; a green short sleeved casual shirt and blue trousers. He is barefoot, a symbol of his humility. Jesus' free hand is uplifted, beckoning. The man's free hand is pointed gingerly towards his own chest as if saying "Me, Lord?" His expression is wide-eyed, beaming hope and faith. He is living James 4:10 "Humble yourselves before the Lord, and He will lift you up." Like the men knocking on the charred tree, he is reaching for a personal relationship with God. But, unlike them, he is reaching for it in his knowledge of Jesus' love and power. And, this man begs God to use him for His purposes.7 The sculpture speaks Isaiah 41:13 "For I am the Lord, your God, who takes hold of your right hand and says to you, Do not fear; I will help you." And also Colossians 3:1 (a) "Since, then, you have been raised with Christ, set your hearts on things above..."

(I ultimately learned the true source of the sculpture. It is a production of Willitts Designs based on the painting "The Invitation" by Morgan Weistling. The scripture of inspiration is Revelations 19:9 NIV "..Blessed are those who are invited to the wedding supper of the Lamb!")

The "ordinary Christians" who are the subjects of these stories are like this man. Their witnessing occurs in many forms, so these testimonials stretch across a broad landscape. None of them asked to be here in these pages; rather, they were selected because they know what it is like to be the person in the statue. The spectrum of their witness is broad: personal counsel, responsible business management, public speaking advice, airport testimonials, and so on.

In today's enormously complicated world, it isn't easy to selflessly make a difference for others. In almost every way, accountability seems increasingly easy to escape.8 While traveling in the American West recently, I crammed a stranded family into my rental car, which already contained a couple of fellow businessmen. After we delivered the unfortunate group to a mechanic, my fellow travelers said "Why did you do that? If we had a wreck, they could have sued you." True enough, I guess, but hardly enough to cause me to leave a family alone in the desert.

Some friends of mine were working with a homeless man who seemed to constantly give away almost everything he touched. Consequently, he was unable to take care of himself and required continual support and ministry. With great understanding, one of the friends interpreted, "He does this because he has no self image." The value of his modesty was subverted because he did not offer himself up to God's use for him, but rather burdened others by his own efforts to escape responsibility. Apparent generosity was actually absent accountability. Unlike the man in the statue, he did not have hold of Jesus' hand. In our interpretation of the scriptures, this is an important distinction to draw. (We will revisit this brother's situation later.)

An important "mission statement" for this text derives from Ephesians 4:29: "Do not let any unwholesome talk come out of your mouths, but only what is helpful for building others up, according to their needs, that it will benefit those who listen." The focus is to build up by seeing the good in others, and in learning the lessons taught by their emulation of Jesus.

In several instances, the subjects of these stories have passed away. In most cases, I had never met their sons and daughters, now mature adults themselves. Certainly, they had no idea who I was. I searched them out to ensure the correctness of my own memories, and to share these stories with them before sharing them with future readers. Often, these actions on their parent's part were heretofore unknown to them. Having a stranger call from "out of the blue" to share these events was often a great source of joy to them and, therefore, a great source of joy to me as well.

Regrettably, I am not able to provide the details of the conversion experiences of all the subjects here. This is especially true of the events in the business realm. For quite some time, this troubled me; how could I say that the individuals were exhibiting Christian behavior when I didn't even know their beliefs? To resolve this, let's spend a few minutes considering the message of a contemporary movie.

TIME CHANGER

While I was in the process of writing this book, some friends and I went to see the movie "Time Changer." If you have not seen it, it should be explained that "Time Changer" is by no means the usual theater fare. It is a decidedly Christian film, spanning the years 1890 to 2002, demonstrating the fate of so called "good principles" when they are separated from Jesus' authority and authorship. The main character, a fictitious author named Russell Carlisle living in the latter part of the 19th century, is consumed with getting his manuscript published (I could relate!). Seeking the endorsement of the seminary at which he is a professor, he faces a tribunal of his peers, one of whom, John Anderson (a character played by Gavin McLeod) is temporarily absent due to a mysterious "illness." It is the requirement of the university that such endorsements require the unanimous approval of all members in attendance; an approval quickly and glowingly granted by those on hand. Then, at the last minute, Anderson enters the room breathlessly and, failing several offers of private counsel with Carlisle, announces that he cannot grant his approval unless a change is made to one small section of the book. The offending piece involves the premise that one should preach good deeds even if doing so means omitting reference to Jesus. An increasingly contentious verbal battle ensues. Carlisle ultimately tries to find ways to circumvent the "unanimity" rule (a morality play in itself) and spurns offers to come to Anderson's home for a clearer explanation of his objection.9

Ultimately, Carlisle relents. Anderson takes him to his barn, where there is a time machine. Carlisle is transported to the future (the year 2002), a trip Anderson had made earlier, with the promise of return in several days. Hungry, he soon buys a hot dog, which is quickly stolen by a little girl. After a comical stiff-legged chase, he catches the girl, recovers his meal, and tells her it is wrong to steal. "*Who* says so?" she replies.

Visiting a laundromat, Carlisle strikes up a friendship with a Hispanic American named Eddie. Eddie constantly refers to himself in the third person as a "good guy" ("Everybody knows Eddie is a good guy") but eschews Carlisle's offers to read the Bible together or participate in church worship activities.

Dozens of new characters and scenarios follow, each portraying values lost over a century of declining emphasis on Jesus as the "author of goodness." On one late evening, Carlisle frustratingly looks at his watch while observing a group of restless cellphone-wielding teenagers. He laments a doorman's casual treatment of divorce, saddened by the man's lack of commitment ("She bugged me, man, so I just dumped her."). He is prevented from making reference to Jesus while speaking at a public function. Rushing out of a theater where several Christians have joined to watch a movie, he is amazed that no one is offended by an actor's onscreen use of the Lord's name in vain.

Interestingly, the filmmakers seldom if ever resort to what we commonly perceive as the "true evils" of our society, drugs, business crimes, political corruption, and so on.10 Rather, the characters in the movie indeed basically seem like "good people," but they have clearly lost their way. Most of the time, they seem to be going through the motions of living their faith

Following these experiences, a very sobered Carlisle returns home and willingly recants his position with respect to changing his manuscript.11

Of course, like Carlisle, as Christians we detest these changes in our values. Our mission is to preserve attribution to Jesus as the source of our good works. But, likewise, we often have to deal with modern restrictions which result in godly works being carried out without the performers being able to publicly speak Christ's name. This is especially true in the school or workplace. For example, in the chapter called *Stones,* I mention a business article that I wrote where I was unable to make reference to Jesus as the inspiration for my actions. Consequently, and sadly, every act lifted up here was not announced as being "in Jesus' name" at the time of the act.

As stated above, for a long time, this troubled me. Then I realized that God was providing me an opportunity that was not provided to some of the participants in these testimonials. These men and women did not have my luxury of separating themselves from their immediate environment to make a movie or write a book. It was left for me to take their example and demonstrate the scriptural principles involved. .12

MERE BROKENNESS—ENOUGH?

Let's revisit our unfortunate homeless brother from page 3. We all know people like him, don't we? We might imagine that he would justify his outlook by the oft-quoted Beatitude verses Matthew 5:3 "Blessed are the poor in spirit, for theirs is the kingdom of heaven" and 5:5 "Blessed are the meek, for they shall inherit the earth." Standing alone, are "poorness in spirit" or "meekness" (perhaps caused by brokenness) enough to induce the kind of behavior that leads to great faith and valuable works? The footnotes in the NIV Full Study Bible (Zondervan) go on to answer this. As "poor in spirit," by definition we "must recognize that we are not spiritually self-sufficient." However, we should also pro-actively *seek* "the Holy Spirit's life, *power* and sustaining grace in order to inherit God's kingdom." "The meek are indeed those who are "humble and submissive…" but the footnote goes on to say that they are also "more concerned about God's *work* and God's people than about what might happen to them personally." Meekness and poorness of spirit are not to be static; they are to induce *dynamic* behavior to grow and serve the Lord, the reaching out for Jesus' hand as the man in the statue. This contrasts to the stagnant and consuming behavior of the brother above, whose brokenness served only to make him constantly draw sustenance from others.

There is a lot of brokenness in evidence in the personal

stories that follow. But mere brokenness is clearly not enough, and solace in verses on meekness alone will hardly permit us to fulfill God's plan as prescribed in the related verses. It is the application of these other bedrock verses that permit us to pick up, drive on and grow. In other words, to put "feet to our faith."

For example, the next Beatitude verse (Matthew 5:6) expands into the dynamic verbiage "Blessed are those who *hunger and thirst for righteousness,* for they will be filled." The corresponding footnote explains that this is one of the most important verses of the Sermon on the Mount. "The foundational requirement for all godly living is to hunger and thirst for righteousness."

Ephesians 3:20 carries the thread to the realm of prayer; "Now to Him (God) who is able to do immeasurably more than all we can ask, or imagine, according to his *power* that is *at work within us.*" And, John 15:16; "I—appointed you to *go and bear fruit,* fruit that will last." The commands to pass beyond mere humility are clear.

MAC

Mac worked with me as one of my managers, but the richest part of our relationship was the matters of faith we shared. Although he attended a different church than I did, he helped out with many of our missions at Warren Baptist Church in Augusta, GA, for example our "Single Mother's Oil Change."13 Mac and I were fortunate to work for a company that did not discourage the prudent sharing of God's love in the workplace, and doing so clearly enhanced our professional relationship and productivity.

Early in our relationship, Mac professed to me a fear of speaking in public, a skill he would ultimately need in the job. Under his own initiative, he tackled and conquered his fears, especially when it came to doing business presentations.14 Then, one day he approached me about a different challenge, one that seemed so "easy" on the surface but underneath was one of the toughest of all. He was asked to give his salvation testimonial to the youth in his congregation. He shared with me the material below, which was ultimately shared with young people in an entirely different way than he planned. Having received Mac's permission to do so, I read his testimonial to the 10th grade boy's Sunday School class that I was struggling to teach, and it helped me overcome some of my own fears.15 Returning to the office Monday morning, I asked him how things went, to which he responded that *his* talk had been cancelled. He was glad to know that God had arranged for the message to be delivered anyway.

"I've been a member here for three and a half years now. I know some of you out there, and recognize many of the faces of most of you. I hope to get to know you all better in the future.

Growing up, no one in my family had much of an interest in church except my grandmother who read the Bible every day. We would go as a family on holidays and occasionally when we could all get up together in time, but for the most part if there was something else to do (like play golf), then that's what we were doing.

I first made a commitment to Christ in college. My best friend and I roomed together. He was a Christian and was constantly hammering away at me to make a commitment. I had always played the devil's advocate to his Christian point of view. I finally committed. I got involved with the Methodist and Baptist groups on campus. But I oscillated and wavered and sat on the fence. It was always about me, enjoying myself, my pleasure. Not to glorify sin, but I did drugs, alcohol, and was very promiscuous. I just didn't care. I basically thought I was invincible. I thought I was the coolest thing since white bread. But I was also constantly hiding things from myself and everyone else. I didn't want anyone knowing that I did certain things. My friend was confident; I was not. He got his confidence from the knowledge that he knew Jesus Christ. In the back of my mind though, I kept telling myself I was a Christian. I kept this lifestyle up until about 10 years ago when my dad was diagnosed with liver cancer. He lived for four months going through chemo. He died in his own bed with his family holding him. I realized at that point how finite life was and is. I wasn't invincible; I wasn't the greatest guy alive. And anyway, who cares? At about that same time, I met my wife who was going through trials of her own. I am convinced the Lord brought us together to work with each other. She has helped me so much. We have both re-dedicated ourselves to Christ. It's not easy. Every day I'm tempted. I struggle all the time, but I know that Jesus Christ is always there with me. When I lost my job almost two years ago, I learned the power that prayer has. I never believed it to be true before, but so many people prayed for our family and so many prayers were answered, I am now a firm believer in prayer.

You have to surrender yourself to Jesus Christ in order to follow Jesus Christ. Being a Christian is hard, hard work. But giving in to sin is the easiest excuse in the world. It takes no guts, no strength and no courage to do the wrong thing. We have free will. And if we choose, we have the grace of a living GOD who has given us a magnificent gift."

The Scriptural View

This is perhaps the most down-to-earth narrative of the stories presented in these pages and, therefore, perhaps the most humble. But the story also unfolds the message of humility being the seed of Christian service. In simple straightforward words, Mac clearly maps his journey from brokenness to his role as a powerful witness for Jesus Christ, overcoming a huge fear (of public speaking) as a result.

We see, in the story and parallel scripture, meekness tied to action. Mac's surrender to Jesus contained elements of several actions. For example, the act of trust, as in Zephaniah 3:12, where the prophet says, "...I will leave within you the meek and humble who *trust* in the name of the Lord." In Psalms

119:67, the act of obedience; David said, "Before I was afflicted, I went astray, but now I *obey* your word." Perhaps 2 Chronicles 7:14 is the most complete and succinct applicable scripture. The Lord spoke to Solomon these words "If my people, who are called by my name, will humble themselves and *pray* and *seek my face* and *turn* from their wicked ways, then will I hear from heaven and will forgive their sin and will heal their land." The powerful bond between these Old Testament verses, Mac's testimony, and Jesus' words in the Beatitudes is crystal clear.

Several statements by Christian philosophers also come to mind; Andrew Murray's "We can never have more of true faith than we have of true humility," D. L. Moody's "The Christian on his knees sees more than the philosopher on tiptoe," and A. W. Tozer's "I believe God will never use anyone that He has not broken deeply." The Moody statement, in particular, evokes he man in the *Invitation* sculpture.

For one final parallel, we turn to Matthew 18:4 "Therefore, whoever humbles himself like this child is the greatest in the kingdom of heaven." And, indeed, Mac was but a child in the early part of his testimony. But he was a child who found growth, first by being prone before his God, and secondly by applying his free will to lifting himself spiritually.

MISSIONARIES AND MENTORS

This book is essentially divided into two categories: the testimonials of those serving in church-supported mission work, and the testimonials of those serving in a different mission field: the workplace. The latter group displays a deep dedication to achieving resonance between their God and their secular profession. That resonance is not intended to be a *mixture* of God and work, but rather that the former will rule the latter. Sometimes, the two worlds of church mission and business intertwine, as in the chapter above and the one entitled *Taxi Robert*. In my life, they have intertwined often.

The mission stories most often involve my fellow congregants at Warren Baptist Church in Augusta, GA, College Park Baptist Church in Greensboro, NC, and First United Methodist Church in Franklin, TN; places where I was blessed to be surrounded by believers who set good examples for me. The Warren experiences, for the most part, occurred following divorce from my marriage of 25 years, a period in which I had to learn to "live" all over again.

The business stories, as mentioned in the introduction, usually involve management or human relations lessons I learned in professional workplaces, from the godly examples of others. All of these experiences occurred in the field of business credit, the field that seemed to choose me more than me it. My friends in other disciplines often tell me "I wouldn't have your job"; the world of business credit is pretty tough. But it therefore makes a pretty good crucible for lesson learning. Along the way, I eventually learned enough from these men and women to contribute, here, some lessons of my own.

Those business experiences were the first seeds of this book. However, when I made early attempts to translate the lessons into a *business* textbook, God tugged at my arm (through the movie "Time Changer") and reminded me of the limitations of this approach. I would not be able to attribute the stories to His Son in that format. So, although I had been rather successful in the field of business publication, I would have to cross into a new realm to get these stories told *the right way*.

Some people refer to those dimly remembered "old days" when being a boss by itself *may* have been enough to command respect, but those days are long gone if indeed they ever existed. Managers today have to do more than ever to earn respect. For example, regardless of one's industry knowledge, being a boss without contemporary computer skills is surely an invitation for scorn from younger workers. Also, such ignorance puts the manager at the disadvantage of being unable to know how long it really takes workers to perform their tasks.

Nonetheless, the major requirement for being responsible for others lives and careers is still this: *character*. This might be stated other ways, or broken into its parts: *maturity, emotional stability, morality, ethics, professionalism, respect for others,* and so on. Somewhere in the mix must be the capability for *tough love*. Neither experience, technical skills, industry knowledge, or any other factor stand as tall as character or, when connected to Jesus' teachings, is as close to godliness. It is character that speaks the loudest in the narratives that follow.

"LUKE"

As a young adult in business I was considerably "overzealous and misdirected" (the favored phrase of my upper management for people like me). I often tried to accomplish some unrealistic selfish objectives, believing I could actually accomplish those things by sheer force of will. This often got me on the wrong side of customers and fellow associates. On most occasions, this gave my superiors, who were politically much brighter than me, a great chance to shine as they stepped in as the guys in the "white hats." This left them looking pretty good and left me flattened in the process. While that by itself provided plenty of learning opportunities for me in the field of human relations, one particular experience was entirely different, and absolutely unforgettable.

I had gotten into a difference of opinion with a customer, a business owner. In my emotion, I disregarded a number of viable alternate solutions to the problem at hand. Our conversation ended unresolved and acrimonious. A few days passed by, and I pretty much forgot about it until the phone rang one morning. The voice on the other line said, "Norm, this is 'Luke.'" Now, I didn't recognize the voice, and I didn't know *anybody* named "Luke." Or at least I didn't think I did. As I thought about it a minute, I realized that the caller was probably Mr. Ed Lucas, Executive Vice President of my employer, and a most important man in the industry. We had never spoken to each other before about anything. With trembling voice I said "Yes Mr. Lucas?" to which he replied "Oh Norm, just call me 'Luke.'" The rest of the conversation revealed that the businessman had called "Kim" (the corporate president) to complain about my decision (and probably tone), and that Kim had asked Ed to handle it. Ed politely asked me what happened and, with increasingly quivering voice I tried to explain the sequence of events. There could be no question that Mr. Lucas was fully aware from my tone that I *knew* I was wrong in my handling of the account. Nonetheless, when I finished, he graciously said, "So heck, we might lose money here if we just let him do what he wants, right? What options do we have?" At which point I was able to lay out the choices that had occurred to me after the conversation with the customer. To my shock Mr. Lucas opined that those were great ideas and asked me to write a letter to the customer offering the alternatives, with a copy to him and my immediate boss.

I penned a softly toned letter. In a few days, I received back from Ed a copy of my letter, with his comments "Norm, this is a great letter and I think you did a nice job calming down a guy who was kinda mad when he called here—Luke." He had sent these comments to my immediate boss as well. Shortly after, the customer and I spoke again, he chose one of the options, peace was made, and thereafter we had a nice mutually profitable relationship.

Several years later, following his retirement, Mr. Lucas had a severe heart attack. I was fortunate that a friend of mine, a therapist, worked with him in his rehabilitation and told me how to get in touch with him. While he was in the hospital, I went to the store and bought a "get well" card. Inside I briefly recounted the above events and told him I never forgot the grace with which he handled the situation. In a few days, the phone rang and my secretary, with puzzled face, looked at me and said, "It's someone named Luke." The voice on the other line, physically weakened yet still full of character, thanked me for the card and reminded me again what a "great job" I did making peace and saving the account.

A few days later, Mr. Lucas passed away.

The Scriptural View

The results of the disparate approaches to the problem (my approach versus Mr. Lucas's) were a clear application of James 4:6 (b) "God opposes the proud and gives grace to the humble."

Our errors can provide others with the opportunity for political gain. By the same token, errors made by those who work for us can provide us with the temptation to gain at their expense.

Ed Lucas was not troubled by such concerns. He saw, in the security of his own abilities and, fortified by his humility, an opportunity to help an embarrassed young professional. What he accomplished in a short phone call, and a few subsequent actions, allowed me to "save face." More importantly, it put me back in direct relationship with the customer. Did he do this to save himself the work of having to personally deal with the man in the future? Of course not. He did it in the highest sense of grace, delegation and empowerment. With no interest whatsoever in his own gain, he displayed a form of Christian managerial love that surely evidenced the phrase "What Would Jesus Do?" For parallels, we can look to Jesus' handling of his impetuous servant Peter in Matthew 26:52, John 18:10-11, Matthew 14:22-31, and Matthew 17:24-27 (like me, Peter needed to be bailed out a lot!); the adulterous woman in John

8:1-11; His mother Mary in John 2:1-11; the Canaanite woman in Matthew 15:21-28; Matthew in Matthew 9:9-13; and the afflicted but faithful in Matthew 9:18-32.

We turn here to another obvious Beatitude, Matthew 5:9, "Blessed are the peacemakers, for they will be called the sons of God. They will strive by their witness and life to bring others, including their enemies, to a peace with God." As the New Oxford Annotated Bible explains, peacemakers are not merely "peace-able," but rather those who "earnestly seek to *make* peace." How much more appropriate, then, could this verse be, with its action verbs "strive" and "bring"? Again we see the bridge from the passive to the active, inherent here in the word "peace*maker*." The latter half of the word denotes the action that turned a personal attribute into a work for God.

To further understand how Christ's examples can influence us in the workplace, let's consider some things that are often overlooked in His approach to ministry. Let's look at how Jesus carried out His own role as a *manager* of others.

JESUS THE MANAGER

I recently asked my 10th grade boys Sunday School students to describe the attributes they recognized in Jesus' life and works. They offered up the following: kindness, forgiveness, healing powers, gentleness, compassion. Those were all true and wonderful, I agreed, but I pointed out to them that they were missing a huge piece of His message to us. I wrote on the chalkboard several additional words. First, *boldness*. Then: *leader, manager, recruiter, delegator, instrument of change.*

Like so many of us, the students had properly recognized Jesus' tender side; the eternal mental images of Jesus with children, the sick, the hungry. They were missing the magnificent power of a different kind: the power to move and motivate others, to assess and utilize their skills, to cause change in established but unethical practices. The kind of power which, if we follow His example, can make an enormous difference in the lives of those around us, as well as our own. And, power which can manifest itself for the forces of good in the workplace.

Consider first the talents and ambitions of the men chosen by Jesus as disciples to carry forth his cause, or who carried it forth shortly afterwards. These are men who, by the first century A. D. had brought the Word to a major portion of the learned world.16 Simon Peter and his brother Andrew, James and John (the sons of Zebedee) were fishermen. Paul was a tentmaker who had at least one second occupation, persecuting Christians. Luke was a doctor. Matthew was, as is well known, a tax collector. The professions of Judas Iscariot, James the son of Alphaeus and his son Thaddeus (also called Judas), Philip, Bartolomew, Thomas, and Simon the Zealot (Simon Peter) were unknown, but apparently they served in jobs that did not require much in the way of leadership skills.

For me, putting this in perspective requires just one simple thought: a reflection on my own tutoring efforts. A couple of years ago, I offered to teach an accounting class to my staff at work. It was a diverse group. On one end of the spectrum were those who were perhaps more knowledgeable in the subject than was I. On the other end were those who simply would never be able to comprehend the material. I remember what a terrible struggle it was to draw a line down the middle, to reach both ends and all those in between. On some minor scale, I succeeded in conveying a few simple concepts to the latter group. I doubt that the former group got much of anything from me. It's not that I was incompetent for the task; I knew the material and had developed capable teaching skills. The simple weight of trying to spread the effort across such a diverse group was, by itself, extremely demanding for me.

Now, imagine that instead of teaching some straightforward accounting rules, you are trying to teach a varied group like the disciples to change the world. As James Hind observed "Christ recruited, trained and motivated twelve ordinary men to become extraordinary. Despite their many shortcomings— their diverse personalities, different appetites and ambitions, and internal disagreements—Christ molded and shaped this group into a 'glorious company.'"

What these men produced can be described no better than the words in an old book I found on a coffee table in the Baptist mission house in Quito, Ecuador. As our mission team settled down for the evening, I was drawn first to the title of the manuscript *The World's Great Religions*.17 (My first reaction was an objection to the plurality in the title.) Under the chapter on Christianity, Paul Hutchinson summed up the growth of our faith quite succinctly:

"The churches in which Christians worship have, during the nearly 2000 years since Christ lived and died, developed such an astonishing diversity of belief and ritual that it is sometimes difficult to recognize that they all acknowledge the same Lord. The glittering spectacle of an Easter Mass in St. Peters, the stillness within the walls of a Quaker meeting house, the squatting circle of Congo tribesmen around the white haired medical missionary, the chanting monks cut off from the world on the forbidden peak of Mt. Athos,18 a hundred thousand Mar Thoma devotees gathered in a dry river bed to join their prayers under the blazing sun of South India, thousands pressing forward in Wembley Stadium to the appeal of an evangelist, wraithlike figures kneeling in perpetual adoration before the alter in a Quebec convent, a sea of dark faces swaying while the tide of the spiritual rolls across them: "It's me, it's me, it's me, o' Lord, standin' in the need of prayer,"—how can these, and hundreds of other differing manifestations, all be accounted as parts of the whole to which we give the name Christianity?"

And yet, surely they are all parts of the whole, a testimonial to those who grabbed Jesus' outstretched hand and spread his word over these 2000 years. Hutchinson later makes reference to a contemporaneous cartoon, which shows a matron in a bookstore asking for "an impartial history of the Civil War written from the Southern point of view." His point, of course, is that any Southerner would argue the Southern cause with enormous passion. The men and women whose lives produced the Christian diversity described above, and their successors, would all the more passionately argue the cause of Christ.

Hind went on to attribute Jesus' success as a manager to, primarily, a "corporate culture that was built around care and concern for others, not himself" through Jesus' promotion and application of "humility of heart." Hind insightfully saw that Jesus exercised the following skills in His management style:

- Discernment, in the form of attention to the individual strengths and weaknesses of the disciples. This permitted:
  - Recognition and development of Peter's leadership skills, partly by harnessing his overreaching and self-assertive nature (as we saw above).
  - Turning the low-profile Andrew into a facilitator who gave others access to Jesus at just the right time. This turned the otherwise timid Andrew into a useful tool.
  - Converting "doubting Thomas" into "doubtless Thomas" and a "confrontive Simon the Zealot into a cooperative disciple" (all managers would appreciate this ability to turn potential malcontents into true believers in the corporate cause).
  - Making an example of Nathanael (Bartholomew), by lauding his great integrity and sincerity.
  - Achieving a complete turnaround with Matthew by changing his focus from accumulation of riches to being a chronicler of Jesus' words.

- Exercising tough love by:
  - Holding His followers accountable for poor performances (Peter's sleeping, James and John's selfishness, Judas' betrayal)—the "tough" part, while
  - Still providing the softness, feeling and generosity associated with "love."

Hind explains that servant leadership does not translate to subservience. Managers should challenge themselves to develop subordinates by helping them thrive and flourish, rather than by "know it all" attitudes. Neither does a "servant management" method "abolish the necessary demands a good manager must place upon others, such as competency, obedience, discipline and hard work." In so doing, managers will bring success upon themselves, but by considering the needs of others first.

This approach, by no means, provides assurance of success in "climbing the corporate ladder." However, it has been interesting for me to watch, with the compaction of corporate pyramids during the last decade, how opportunities have been provided for those who closely follow Jesus' style. The elimination of clouding structures has laid us all bare, providing those who are able to exercise broad and selfless developmental skills with better chances to show their wares. My favorite example is a friend, Ron, whose name once appeared in fine print on a lower level of a huge organizational chart for a major firm. Although blessed with enormous "people" and organizational skills, he remained submerged there, shuffling around beneath managers who were perhaps more "polished", until his company "went private."19 The elimination of positions that were peopled by those who had become wealthy and perhaps lost their drive exposed his abilities. In a few years, his supervision stretched much further than that of his predecessors. He became the embodiment of humility set free to spread its wings in the workplace.

ECUADOR

Warren Baptist Church makes regular mission trips to essentially every part of the globe; China, Russia, Cypress, South America, Scotland, and Conyers, Georgia. Conyers, Georgia, outside of Atlanta? We forget sometimes, we are just as much missionaries near to home as we are far away, if anything, more so.

Our Minister of Missions, and leader of these trips, is a man of solid proportions named Roger Henderson. His respect for his physical body is clear testimonial to 1 Corinthians 6:19 ".. your body is a temple of the Holy Spirit" and Romans 12:1 "Therefore, brothers,...I urge you to present your bodies as a living sacrifice, holy and pleasing to God; this is your spiritual worship." Roger is a marathon runner, although he will readily admit he does not look the part. With his typical beaming smile and "good sport" personality, he explains that he is technically in a class of runners called "Clydesdales." His heart for the Lord is as impressive as his physical presence. Cherubic greetings, twinkling eyes and warm bear hugs personify Roger. All this said, perhaps his strongest traits are the organizational and leadership skills so necessary to carry off such large endeavors; talents that are representative of Jesus as Manager.

Because I travel Latin America frequently in my profession, when I received God's call to make a mission trip, I chose Ecuador. Carrying along large plastic crates filled with power tools and medical supplies, our team (38 people aged 10 years to 65 years) headed south in June of 2002. We had a big job ahead of us, medical and dental maintenance for hundreds of people, heavy and complicated carpentry work, carrying the witness of Jesus with us while performing these tasks.20 With the heightened security in the wake of the tragedies of September 11, 2001, we were subject to heavy scrutiny at the airports and immigration points. Somehow, the entire row of six passengers where I was seated on the outbound plane was selected for "random" searches. This attachment stayed with us throughout the trip, and we grew pretty weary of having to open up our baggage at every possible checkpoint.

The country's name is Spanish for "Equator," as indeed that meridian saws through the heart of the nation. Those expecting temperatures commensurate with the name were surprised, as the altitude of the places we visited made it quite cold even in late spring. One of our few tourist stops included the *old* "Center of the World."21 In the courtyard of a little village, a tarnished brass strip bisects a flat round concrete base topped by a globe. In the ultimate photo opportunity, we took turns straddling the dividing line, standing in both hemispheres at once. We became obsessed with verifying the Coriolis force, the physics that cause water in basins to drain clockwise in the North and counterclockwise in the South. Nearby bathrooms confirmed this, prompting some humorous disagreements throughout the balance of the trip as to why this happens.

An unpleasant discovery, for those of us without foreknowledge, is the countrywide constriction that prohibits the flushing of toilet paper. This is due to a literal plumbing constriction; the PVC pipes used in Ecuador are too narrow to permit the paper to pass. Instead, the user simply places the material in a hooded basket located in the stall. This takes a day or two to get used to.

In so many ways, the touch of industrial man has sullied the natural beauty of this otherwise lovely country. The cities are unattractive to our eyes; I scarcely saw any structure that I thought was architecturally appealing. Hardly any building seems finished; yards cluttered with wheelbarrows full of concrete, countless spires of rusty steel rebar point skyward.22

The countryside is an entirely different matter. In a vehicle the size of a typical tour bus, we traveled narrow mountainside roads to the villages at 12,000 feet. In the frequent hairpin turns, the roadbed vanished under the sides of the bus, leaving me peering down uncomfortably at nothing but cliff face. Except for an enormous nursery we passed on the way, I scarcely saw a flat place in all of Ecuador.23 The volcanic soil, a six foot depth of rich black earth, is cultivated everywhere it can possibly be tilled, to inclinations as steep as 70 degrees, where adz-shaped hand tillers are used. The result is a patchwork quilt landscape in infinite shades of green and brown.

At the mountaintop,24 we sequestered part of a building similar to an American "strip" shopping mall, a linear structure that housed a sequence of rooms. (It reminded me of the shopping area in my birthplace of Oakton, Kentucky.) The rooms were very sparsely furnished; one was used as a rudimentary school. The native Quechua (kee-choo-wa) Indian people gathered quickly as word spread that our team had returned for our annual spiritual and medical ministries. The people are small of stature, a function of genetics and diet.25 Regardless of gender, all wore men's fedoras against the cold. The ladies were dressed in brightly colored native dress. On the men's clothing, occasionally the words "Gap," "Old Navy," and "Nike" appeared. The Quechua are, of course, generally oblivious to the significance of these names or the millions of dollars spent promoting them. (Unlike some Latin countries, Ecuador has not yet developed much of an apparel manufacturing base. In a few scant years, proposed trade pacts may move thousands of these natives into factories where their lives will be forever changed and their livelihoods will depend on these labels.)

Having no medical skills, my assignment was to witness to those awaiting care, as best I could, despite what I learned was a *multiple* language barrier. I had brought with me some "EvangeCubes"; puzzle shaped blocks where the message of the Gospels unfolds in pictures.[26] The Ecuadorian lay missionaries who traveled with us from Quito held the instruction sheet for me as I read the corresponding messages in my pigeon Spanish. Confused looks were returned from the seated natives. One particular man smiled broadly at me, impishly sympathizing with my ignorance. Many Quechua, especially the ladies, spoke no Spanish, only the local version of the Quechua tongue (there are many versions throughout South America). Resolved to help me, his eyes fixed to mine and, as I spoke the Spanish words, "Jesucristo" for "Jesus" and so on, he interpreted for me.

An incredible aspect of the human spirit, to me, is our ability to understand each other despite enormous language barriers. As we did carpentry work on a 400-year-old church in downtown Quito,[27] it was a great thrill to me to eventually make lone forays to the local shops in search of equipment and supplies.[28] (Incredibly, the original explorers of the Australian interior, Burke and Wills, died of starvation in the midst of indigenous populations, arrogantly drifting away from these potential rescuers despite their increasingly tragic situation.[29]) I have had many rewarding bilingual communication experiences in the business realm, finding that even difficult accounting concepts can be shared with just a few common words. Sharing the Lord in this fashion was infinitely more satisfying. The eyes of the natives were huge with desire for our message; people ran to us as they saw us minister. Ultimately, one of the local lay ministers, Alejandro Cacuango from King's church, came to my aid and handled the verbal part, as I worked the cube. I will never forget his passion. He would turn to the words on the card, then turn back to the native to whom he was witnessing, his whole being (arms, hands, speech) consumed in the Word.

The members of our medical team worked hard in the challenging cold and altitude. Tuesday was special, 234 people were ministered to in the mountains. Having served down in the church that day, rather than in the villages, I could only experience their fatigue by looking into their cold and tired faces as they returned to the mission house in the evening. Even the ever-cheerful pharmacist Dave Killough, who always seemed to wear a baseball cap backwards, could barely muster a smile.

The Quito congregation welcomed us to one of their worship services (in true Southern Baptist tradition, on a Wednesday night). The musical portion of a Quechua service consists of selections from their 400 or so hymns, but there are only five or six tunes for these hymns (all undistinguishable from each other, to my ears). The instrumentation consisted of a drum kit and a portable electric keyboard that seemed incapable of producing anything but high notes. This melded perfectly with the singing. Although the membership consisted of male and female adults and children, the effect was one voice, lilting and birdlike, feminine, childlike, and entirely captivating. As a special treat, the women's choir performed for us. The twelve ladies, in two tiers of six, performed several of their hymns for us. They had adorned themselves in their finest native attire, and were properly hatless in the sanctuary. Many of them were understandably sensitive to our presence and, in their shyness, they were unable to make eye contact with us. As the evening progressed, I found opportunities to exchange, via handshakes, a few five-dollar bills with the local men who had helped us with the church repairs. Unlike some cultures in the Latin world, the Quechua custom did not seem to welcome men hugging men. The gift produced an exception, along with a look of appreciation far beyond what the small token should have earned (although, of course, five dollars of American money is probably more appreciated there than here at home).30

Receiving such intense appreciation and modesty seemed, if anything, unfounded to me, and made me want to return the sentiments in increased measure. I couldn't help but think, if we removed our offerings of Savior and medical supplies, would a gift of the basic American lifestyle be much of a blessing to them?31 Our divorce rates, crime rates, the loss of values described in "Time Changer"? Their passion to know Christ, and to experience Him personally, was written in their eyes. The deep honesty of their spirit was unquestionably present, and present without the slightest hint of equivocation.

In the business world, we often feel encouraged to be evasive, to be guarded about our intentions or beliefs, or to at least hedge our positions. I have several favorite definitions of stress. One is a sweatshirt I saw for sale in a catalog. It read, "Stress is when your stomach says 'No way' and your mouth says 'Of course I'll do it.'" Another opines that stress is the moral difference between what you believe is right and what you find yourself called upon to do in the workplace. It seemed to me that, in the togetherness of families achieving a hard won sustenance from the earth, the Quechua might have a leg or two up on us in that area.

I had always heard that "Going on a mission trip will change your life." Ecuador taught me that this saying has many meanings. To witness to others, you have to be close to Jesus Christ yourself. Those native eyes will see through your lie very quickly if you are not. Those same eyes return values of childlike faith and love, and demonstrate what it is like to have 100% acceptance. In so doing, the intended pupils teach us, completing a circle of Jesus' love. We do not have to travel a long way to see this happen. I experience the very same thing when I participate in one of Robert William's ministries (see chapter on same). But you cannot experience it unless you offer yourself up to it and take His hand.

The Scriptural View

To understand the requirement for us to mirror the Quechua's childlike approach to spirituality, we revisit Matthew 18:4. Perhaps even more relevant to what I personally experienced in Ecuador, consider Jesus' words in Matthew 11:25 and Luke 10:21 "I praise you, Father, Lord of heaven and earth, because you have hidden these things from the wise and learned, and revealed them to little children." In Matthew 18:1-3, when the disciples asked "Who is the greatest in the kingdom of heaven," Jesus replied "I tell you the truth, unless you change and become like little children, you will never enter the kingdom of heaven." Another relevant verse is Isaiah 11:6(b) "...and a little child will lead them."

During my life, I have worked with many very successful salespeople. As I grew to know them personally, I came to realize that they come in all varieties, some avid golfers and some not, some technologically gifted and some technologically challenged, some devoted family men and some not, and on and on. While participating in a work related personality survey, I mentioned this observation to the surveyor. "Is there some kind of common behavioral thread in the sales profession?" I asked her. "Yes," she quickly responded, "it seems that most good salespeople have a high quotient of 'child' in them."

I will, naturally, not categorize evangelism as "selling Jesus." However, we must consider that some of the primary human characteristics involved in spreading the Gospel are common to good salesmanship. For example, creativity and passion are, as the surveyor explained to me, products of a childlike personality. This is never more evident to me than my personal relationship with my friend, Jim Overstreet (see his chapter, *Jim and Bobby*). Jim, as a responsible business owner supporting a family, is by God's gift a salesman of worldly goods. Christlike values and ethics unfold from him, and unfold (he would acknowledge) in a childlike way not unlike the Quechua. And his eyes speak the same spiritual language as the Quechua.

On the day before we returned home, several of us climbed a section of Mount Cotopaxi. Cotopaxi is the second highest "active" volcano in the world (fortunately not very active at this time), having given up the premier position to Chile's Tupungato when the latter became truly active in 1986. (Cotopaxi is approximately the same height as Africa's Mount Kilimanjaro.) We drove to an altitude of 15,000 feet, where there was a small parking area about 100 yards downhill from a shelter. We had rented special gear to wear for our ascent, the objective being a glacier at about 16,500 feet. My own pampered recreational experiences prompted me to ask, "Where do we put on our suits?" Roger pointed down to the gravel at our feet. The high winds at the exposed promontory caused several of us to have to chase down our gloves, sapping much of our energy. None of us had ever been to this altitude before, and we were all laboring to one degree or another. Roger and I were the two oldest members of the group, both 52, but he was in considerably better shape than I. Achieving the shelter required a series of four or five slow steps, a slight slide backward in the gravel, stop, five more steps, until finally Roger and I were first to arrive. This gave me a sense of overconfidence that was flattened a bit later. Getting under way again, Roger and the others made the glacier, put on their crampons and climbed up it a bit. I sat down in snow and rocks slightly below them, completely exhausted, and positioned myself to overlook the quilted valleys and mountains below us. *Now,* the part of God's glory that manifests itself in nature unfolded its full glory below me, with little trace of man's intrusions. The hymn "This is My Father's World" sang in my oxygen starved brain, the skies and rocks and trees spoke to me. "The land produced vegetation; plants bearing seed according to their kinds and trees bearing fruit with seed in it according to their kinds. And God saw that it was good." (Genesis 1:12).

Having recently read Jon Krakauer's *Into Thin Air,* I could now at least modestly relate to the tribulations of the real climbers he described. If anything, the giddiness made the experience unique and enhanced my appreciation of God's handiwork. I got back to the shelter mostly by sticking out my useless legs as weak brakes, sliding on my backside through the snow and loose rock. "From the Lord comes deliverance..." [Psalm 3:8(a)]. "For the Lord is my rock, my fortress, and my deliverer; my God is my rock, in whom I take refuge." [Psalm 18:2 (a)].

The text here on Ecuador, in part, gives worship to

God's beauty as it shows itself in the natural world around us. I wrote much of it in reflection when I visited another scene of such beauty, the Rocky Mountains around Denver, during wintertime. As we drove along the highway between Breckenridge and Vail, I couldn't take my nose off the inside of the passenger car widow. The incredible contrast of the red sandstone buttes as they protruded through the sugar snow, the fuzzy patches of aspens like tan straw needles standing upright among the green lodgepole, ponderosa and bristlecone pines. I once read that the science of geology had been unable to ascertain the source of the Rockies; they are too far from the West Coast to have been produced by plate tectonics. My friend Kevin Beckett (see his chapter) assured me that he knew where (Who) they came from.

All platitudes to the beauty of "Mother Nature" and the spiritual simplicity of the Quechua nature call for a caveat. In the movie *1492,* Gerard Depardieu's Christopher Columbus voices his belief that the Caribbean peoples live in a "Garden of Eden" where nature is their god. This is a frequent observation of many travelers and explorers. But it rings hollow when the sin nature inherent in *all* cultures becomes evident, as inevitably it does. These societies are no less subject to Adam's legacy than are we, and Mother Nature never forgave anyone's sin or provided for their salvation. While nature is one of God's glories, it is but one.

It would be appropriate to close to this section by paying memory to missionary Jim Elliott, and his favorite Bible verse, Exodus 23:20 "I am going to send an angel before you to protect you on the road and to bring you to the place that I have prepared." For Ecuador, Jim was that angel.

CARL BROWN

To envision Carl Brown (now retired), picture a strong, astute man, of average height and sturdy lanterned features, brimming with self-confidence and people skills. Someone who was seldom if ever uneasy, regardless of the pressure of a difficult situation, whose voice was soft but endowed with a slight rasp, whose words were usually issued with deliberate measurement. As my boss, he was the director of an apparel company's credit department in the 1980's. His confidence was reinforced by the support of our Chief Financial Officer. Complaining customers who appealed to the CFO were usually greeted by the response "Mr. Brown's decisions aren't subject to reversal."

Carl always possessed another extremely rare quality: a God given ability to teach a lesson without conveying the slightest concept that he was trying to teach. In fact, his comments made me understand that *he* often didn't realize he was teaching. His abilities came very naturally. When I recently reminisced with him about his days as my boss, he remembered the business part of what he was trying to accomplish (for example, helping a customer save his business) but not the lessons themselves. That seems ironic since, back in those days, I know he was frustrated I didn't catch on. I suppose I'm relieved he's forgotten.

Carl was a "tough love" practitioner, even with himself. The thought that he would receive credit for the sensitive aspects of what he did was completely alien to him. Nonetheless, that credit has to be given.

No one I ever met was better at the protection of someone's image, the keeping of a confidence, or encouragement through kind words that maybe the recipient didn't quite deserve. If that last thing seems out of concert with tough love, I should add that the unearned kind words were for *public* ears. If the underlying performance called for a different approach (i. e. discipline for an error), that lesson was delivered in private.

One of our managers, who we will call "Joe," once got himself into considerably more professional trouble than he could escape, the result of drinking heavily at a company function. The necessary demotion was administered quickly and quietly. Sadly, Joe did not reach up for Jesus' outstretched Hand, although many human agents acted on his behalf. Joe ultimately left the company, went through a regressive series of low-level jobs, and passed away penniless on his houseboat at the age of 55.32 Over the years, many people tried to kindle a conversation with Carl about the incident that necessitated the demotion. Joe's image was always protected. The answer was always the same, even long after Joe's death: a quizzical "what incident?" look and a change of subject.

As I mentioned above, Carl's voice was usually soft and mannered. When it was not, there was a definite purpose behind the clockwise turn of the volume knob. It was akin to the parent's raised eyebrow, the addressing of the child by both his first and middle name.

Bobby Joe was a Texas merchant (yes, that was his real name and home state) whose business acumen fell quite a bit short of his belief in himself. (In other words, he was arrogant.)

He had recently purchased the retail store where he had been employed for several years. The business had been built to a successful level by a much savvier gentleman. As suppliers of product to that business, we were deeply concerned that the new owner would not be able to sustain the existing profitable operation. Still, the order volume with us was very good. So, the overall picture was in shades of gray, and the credit decision was a tough one. Bobby Joe naturally disliked my initial decision, that we would require cash in advance, and probably disliked the way I presented the decision. He appealed to Carl, who agreed to extend a line of credit, whereupon Carl instantly became Bobby Joe's "best friend."

Whenever Bobby Joe called, Carl (whose office was next to mine) spoke a little louder to be sure I could hear the cordial nature of their conversations. I was personally offended that my decision had been reversed, so their relationship irritated me. Professionally, I felt sure we were headed for disaster. I knew that the store was selling our products at essentially breakeven prices and could not survive. Week after week, the sales staff marveled at Carl's relationship with Bobby Joe, and the "permanence" of our dedication to him and his operation.

Then, payments began to slow. I became *convinced* we were headed for disaster. Carl's demeanor remained unchanged. Payments slowed a little more, then a little more. At what I later realized was just the right moment, Carl withdrew credit, and shipments were stopped. Bobby Joe appealed to our CFO, who referred the call back to Carl, with the usual comment "Mr. Brown's decisions aren't subject to reversal." There was no room for appeal, as everyone had come to see Carl as the customer's greatest supporter. Raising his voice for the first time, for my benefit and the customer's, Carl told Bobby Joe that he was pretty bold to take the matter to the CFO, that we needed to be paid on time if we were going to sell him anymore, and so on. Carl stood up, waved his arms, and gestured at the walls. Though he was hundreds of miles away, I could feel Bobby Joe become temporarily lifeless. I could also feel myself learning the lesson I was supposed to learn.

We collected our money and turned the account to cash in advance, taking no loss in the subsequent bankruptcy. This was a much happier outcome, at least for us, than might have been. We could have taken a large bad debt loss. Carl knew he was running a risk but, throughout the process, he weighed the relevant issues and moved accordingly. How much time did we have before likely failure, how much profit were we making with each collection, as opposed to the possible loss, and so on. Early in the process, he got us ahead of the game in the risk/return arena. But his most important move was this: he was taking control of the situation, making sure that, as head of the department, he established himself as the court of last appeal. The buck stopped with Carl. This was a leadership lesson I never forgot. We cannot always have absolutes like complete victory, zero risk, and so on. But we can take the ball, take the responsibility, and guide the ship into the best harbor available. In a corporate world where "Let George do it"33 so often prevails, this is an important lesson to learn.

Obviously there were at least two other lessons in evidence here: the desirability of catching insects with honey instead other materials, and the feeding out of *jussst enoughhhh* rope to accomplish the needed purpose. All the planning and preparation that produced the result were also the manifestation of another of Carl's favorite expressions: "The race ain't necessarily to the swift."

The Scriptural View

At a recent Men's Bible study, the scripture under our discussion was Matthew 21:12, Jesus and the moneychangers. The conversation quickly turned to the subject of anger and lost temper. Some of the men wrestled with Jesus actions, seeing them as evidence that He "lost his temper" because he overturned the tables of the moneychangers and drove them from the temple. Some were afraid this was evidence of sinful behavior; some rationalized it by classifying it as "righteous indignation."

On a hunch, not knowing what the search would reveal, I suggested we pull out all the Bibles in the house and see if any of the interpretations indicated that Jesus had "lost His temper."

None of the translations in any way hinted that Jesus had lost control of himself. Not King James, not New King James, not New International Version, not New American Standard, not New Oxford Annotated, not Revised Standard Version. Each translation simply described Jesus' actions and reason for them.

We had missed the point; the lesson that Carl taught me. A "good manager" (and Jesus certainly was that) need not give way to anger to make his point. Although the voice level may rise and the actions may become demonstrative, emotions should remain under control. If we imperfect humans can accomplish that, surely Jesus could and did.

The lesson here also clearly involved the value of patience. We look to the parallel in Proverbs 19:11 (a) "A man's wisdom gives him patience." And, Ecclesiastes 7:8 (b) "…..patience is better than pride." Carl's patience provided for a successful outcome, in contrast to the ineffectiveness of my vision clouded by wounded pride.

ALEX

Alex's professional star had dimmed considerably by the time I met him. We were both working in the credit department of a huge Fortune 500 company. I was the manager of a portion of the department; Alex worked for one of my peers as a temporary employee hired to help write a few reports. Prior to coming to the company, he had been a highly placed accounting manager for a division of another Fortune 500 firm. When his division was closed down, Alex burned several bridges in his anger and lost an opportunity to be moved to another division. Thus, he wound up with us at, essentially, a clerical level.

The circumstances that placed him in this role aside, Alex was one of the most brilliant people I have ever known. Although he had no formal training in the complicated software that we used, he became our point man to track down all "bugs," a job he handled most capably. His reports were written accurately and with admirable prose. Just as I began to think of him as a master technician, he shared with me his real love: He was a part time minister at a small country church nearby.

Alex's boss was very intimidated by his skills, and Alex did not respect his boss because the gentleman lacked industry experience. Although this feeling seldom revealed itself in dramatic ways, there was always an undercurrent between them. Finally, one day, the department head approached me quietly and asked if he could transfer Alex to my area.

Alex had already shared with me his appreciation for our shared industry experience. I saw my main challenge as getting him to understand that I would react positively to his technical skills, which were far superior to my own.

On the day of the transfer, I assembled my existing team in my office. I sat among the group, beside the collections manager. When Alex entered the office, I asked him to sit in the empty chair behind my desk. When he was comfortable, I welcomed him to the group and asked him, since we had worked closely for two years, what things he had observed that would help our team do a better job. He made a couple of suggestions, which we all opined were good (because they were), and then we all went back to work.

Over the time that Alex and I worked together, I began to realize that his occasional altercations with people almost always involved female professionals. When I approached him about that tendency, his response was straightforward and intriguing. When he was small, his father called the family together, pointed at Alex's mother and said "If she *ever* disciplines you in my absence, I want you to let me know about it when I get home." This caused Alex to occasionally experience emotional struggles when dealing with women in power. Fortunately, he recognized the problem, and the source of it, and therefore was usually able to overcome it.

Alex and I remained close friends throughout our association. He continued to be smarter than me, he continued to understand that I knew and respected that, and he continued to work for me. In a few years, the division was shut down and we all had to find other employment. Today, I am proud to say that he found satisfaction in his true love. He is the successful pastor of a large church in a growing college town.

The Scriptural View

We just can't always be "superior in every way" to those in our care, and we must not let their abilities intimidate us into poor management technique. For the "team" to function well, a good manager will simply recognize, publicly and privately, that person's skills and use them for the greater good of all.

While Jesus surely never encountered anyone "smarter" than He (or superior to him in any way), through His life he constantly encountered those who were equipped with better earthly resources, those with more secular "power." For examples that He set by applying grace to people in such "high places," see the centurion in Matthew 8:5-13, and the High Priest's servant in Matthew 26:50-52 who was endangered by a disciple. Certainly many previously cited examples from the chapter *Jesus the Manager* would also apply here.

However, more the credit is due to Alex himself for having the grace to accept my management of him, exhibiting great humility despite the superiority he possessed in so many areas.

A. J. HEWETT

In his book Wild at Heart, John Eldredge laments the fate of modern man, commenting that one of the aims of contemporary society is to "turn men into women," and the aim of the church is to turn us into "really boring nice guys." He must have never met my friend A. J. Hewett.

I was only privileged to know A. J. for a brief time; the few years before his death at the age of 82. Without question, he was an *important man* by the world's standards; he was wealthy, active in civic affairs, and a prominent local businessman. He was a *man of the church*, serving as a prominent deacon in the place of worship we both attended, which his construction company built. He was a *family man*, married to a beautiful and sweet woman named Ruth and blessed with lovely and successful children. And, he was a *handsome man*, tall, trim, and distinguished in appearance.

Above all this, though, he was simply a *man*; tough and often salty yet at once deeply feeling and caring, all in the same mortal "shell." He was fully capable of calling on whichever resources were needed at the moment. This was always done for the betterment of those around him, perhaps a "tough love" lesson to a young person, a word of encouragement to a friend, whatever the occasion demanded. And, it was always done without a trace of manipulation or cunning; it was just as instinctive to him as breath.

In a recent newspaper article about the late Al McGuire, former college basketball announcer and NCAA championship coach at Marquette, it was said that Al was not so much a *religious man* as he was a *spiritual man*. As I read this, I realized what a perfect characterization it was for A. J. as well.

My favorite memory was the Wednesday night "White Bible" service in honor of his close friend Ken Tutterow's grandson, Alan, and Alan's fiancée Ruthie. Now, for those who are not "old Baptists," a "White Bible" service is one in which engaged couples sit before the congregation and accept their counsel on the issue of marriage. A. J.'s first offering came from his salty side; no need to repeat it here save to say that it brought red cheeks to the ladies, and men as well. I'm not sure anyone else could have said it without being escorted out. Everyone knew that, in time, it would be followed by something the young couple could soak into their hearts as an anchor for their life together. And indeed it was. As the service neared the end, the advice came, with loving voice and tender eye contact: "Alan, Ruthie, if each of you will just give the marriage your share, *and then a little more*, you'll be fine." So many marriages have crumbled in the failing of that simple principle.

As Director of Baptist Men in our church, I spent many a Sunday morning helping prepare the meals for our Men's Breakfast, burning the sausage while watching Buddy Kelly make his championship grits. One of the best parts of the job was the guest speakers I recruited, and their stories. The most memorable were our guests from the *Delancey Street Foundation*, a leading self-help education center for former substance abusers and ex-convicts. My call to their office, to request a "staff member" to speak to our membership, resulted in a sobering response. The lady who answered the phone said, "We don't have any staff, just ex-heroin addicts, cocaine users, alcoholics, prostitutes, and the like." (As the Foundation director Dr. Mimi Silbert says, "People who would be considered patients in other programs are the bosses here.") My entreaties that she think of herself and her fellows more favorably met with her kind yet determined response that she must never forget what she had become, so that she might not continue to be. The two Delancey representatives gave us a Sunday morning lesson on humility that I will never forget.

During these Sunday morning activities, A. J. would usually come in early, so he and I had some time together by ourselves. Like most of us, he would occasionally run afoul of traffic laws, so I sometimes got the benefit of hearing of his treatment at the hands of various local constables. On one particular occasion, while travelling a little too fast in a small Carolinas town, he was "pulled" by a motorcycle patrolman. In great detail, A. J. explained how the officer slowly dismounted his vehicle, patiently removed his long gauntlet gloves, and approached his car. "Mr. Hewett, we have a nice little peaceful town here, with some elderly people and children who often have occasion to cross the streets. I'm not going to give you a ticket today, but the next time you come through our town, I wish you'd think about those folks and how much they mean to us." The message was clear; one that he could and did respect. Conversely, he would sometimes encounter law enforcement officials blessed with a little too much self-importance, to which his response was usually "Just give me the ticket."

During one men's breakfast, my oldest daughter Kelly, aged 3 at the time, had just learned the prayer:

> "What can I give Him, as poor as I am
> If I were a shepherd, I'd give Him a lamb
> If I were a wise man, I'd do my part

But what can I give Him
I'll give Him my heart."

She happened to share it with me just as we began to serve and, my heart bursting with pride in her, I instinctively asked her to say it in grace for the meal. She turned and said "Dad you say it with me," but I couldn't because I didn't know it. Whereupon she did it by herself to the 40 people some odd people gathered there. As I stood there speechless in an unforgettable memory of fatherhood, A. J. quietly walked up to me, put his hand on my shoulder and said "If you keep raising her right like that, she will be someone very very special." In that moment, he forever made me his accountability partner in fatherhood.

Just as his health began to decline, A. J. asked me if he could take a turn addressing the breakfast members. To me, this was a little like a father asking his son for permission to do something. Before I could get him lined up, he was hospitalized, and we were all afraid we would never get to hear the story. Then, the Lord mercifully granted us the great gift of his recovery.

The story that followed dealt with a German prisoner of war named Heinz who, during World War II, was sent to Fort Bragg, North Carolina, and assigned to work for A. J.'s construction company. He told the story of the respect he developed for the young man, and the bond that developed between them as he gave him more and more responsibility in the office. After the war ended, the two men kept in touch with cards and letters for a few years. In early 1970, A. J. and Ruth took a trip to Belgium to visit their daughter, who drove them to Essen, Germany, in the hopes of seeing Heinz and his family. Carrying the last yellowing letter from his friend in his pocket, to A. J.'s surprise, he found that Heinz was still at the same address that appeared on the letter. As they joyfully met in that home, there on the mantelpiece sat A. J.'s own last letter. At that point of the presentation, something happened that very few had ever seen: A. J. cried.

A few months later, his health declined again, and then came the end of his life on earth. Our minister sat by his side in the hospital and helped him fight the battle. After each crisis, Mike would say "Well, A. J., we made it through that!" A. J., realizing the end was near, would simply say "But what next, preacher, what next?"

One night, while visiting several of our church members who were ill, I stopped by A. J.'s room. He was upright in the hospital bed, connected to an array of tubes and other medical apparatuses. At first I thought he was talking to someone, but then I realized we were alone, but he did not know I was there. I left as quickly as I could, as I knew that was not the way he would have wanted any of us to remember him. But I was grieved that I could not have said that one last word of respect I wanted to share with him, as the next day I learned he died that night.

In his eulogy, Mike observed that, as a person approaches death, there are two things he or she wants to know. One, did they make a difference; two, will they be remembered? A. J.'s fulfillment of the former is evident from this story itself; fulfillment of the latter is the cause for it to be recorded.

Mike also told the story of how A. J. came to refer to himself by his initials. His given name was Allen June and, since his mother called him June, so did everyone else. When his college graduation drew near, he sent out resumes to potential employers. One company responded that, while his credentials were excellent, they regretted to advise him that they did not hire women. On that day, June Hewett became A. J. Hewett. And we can only imagine what his other reactions were to that response!

(Thanks to Robert Hewett, A. J.'s son, for filling in some important details in the construction of this story, and for his joy in sharing these recollections of A. J.'s life and testimony)

"Wet Sand"

There is always a great temptation to try to emulate someone we admire; in the way I admired A. J. (In other words, to put into practice A. W. Tozer's theory that "Nearness is likeness.") The danger is that we will wind up with a personal dichotomy. A. J.'s many admirable qualities, his broad personality, the ability to be both tender and firm, were a natural part of his personal chemistry, his upbringing, and other factors. Any other given person is obviously "keypunched" at least somewhat differently. Therefore, any effort to "become more like" some other human is going to provide some significant adaptation challenges. Anyone naturally inclined to strength in dealing firmly with others may have trouble with sensitivity, and vice versa.

As a child, on a visit to the beach, I tried to make a sandcastle from dry sand that I had put in a bucket and doused with seawater. Lower down on the beach, an adult was making a similar castle. As mine crumbled, and his stood tall, he explained to me that he was making a castle from *wet sand* while I was making a castle from sand I had *made wet*.

Our personalities are sometimes a bit like that sand that was *made wet*. That is, we may not have enjoyed the factors that seem to naturally produce the strength of spirit, the faith, the

Godliness that we observe in others. We may struggle to put this "good stuff" inside us, all the while wrestling with our own individual sin natures. We may feel that we have much more façade than foundation. As a friend of mine describes it, we may feel that we have to "Fake it til we make it," that is, let our works lead us as we struggle toward a stronger faith. But such an approach, as Dr. David Fleming reminded us in a recent sermon, represents an *imitation* (on the outside) that is still searching for an *incarnation* (on the inside).

Through this battle, as much as we may admire any other given human, we must look to the ultimate "wet sand": Jesus Christ. As long as we simply try to be "like someone else (some other person)," we will always miss the point and forget that person has his or her wrestlings with sin just like we do (see *The Seamstress*). Rather, by looking upward to Jesus (and grabbing His hand), instead of sideways to another person, we can find the proper role model for spiritual foundation. A. J. certainly understood and appreciated this, and quoted the same source for his own strengths.

CREDERE

In June of 2002, the magazine "Credit Today" ran a contest for the "Best Credit Decision of the Year." I wanted to enter, but I had suffered a particularly bad year, with heavy bad debt losses in the economic wake of the events of September 11, 2001. Consequently, I didn't think I had any good stories to tell. Then I remembered something I had seen many times in my business classes, that the Latin root of the word "credit" is "credere" or "to trust." The decision didn't need to be one in which I escaped a loss from a company that failed, it could just as easily be one where trust was rewarded by having faith in someone who succeeded despite heavy hardships. In other words, a story involving character. At the last minute, following prayer on the matter, I submitted the following story:

Let's think a minute about what constitutes a "good (or great) credit decision." Obviously, it ought to be one where you collected your money, or at least ultimately generated a desirable return on the money you put at risk. Also, to be a really outstanding decision, it ought to be one where you took a material amount of risk for good reason and wound up being justified in doing so. It should be a "team" decision, in which you brought in the key players in your organization and asked for their input. And one in which you considered all the impacts on your organization: the risk/return scenario over time, the profitability of keeping a plant running versus the expense of curtailments (including restaffing and retraining after shutdown), and so forth. One in which the time was taken to make a personal visit to meet the individuals involved and to understand the operation. And, to me, it ought to be a decision where the *character* of the customer's management played a major role, not just the numbers on a piece of paper.

Like many industries, the American textile business has been under major siege, for many years, by overseas competition. As managers, we have an enormous responsibility to not only our industries but also our country to find ways to keep manufacturing on these shores and keep our workers employed. "Good credit decisions" play a huge role in that process, much larger than the average person understands.

The customer in this story was (undisclosed) an active account with my company for many years. As they encountered financial problems which then worsened, we began to draw down our exposures to them. Ultimately, this prompted a call from our Vice President of Yarn Sales, asking me for a re-assessment. He needed a $350,000 credit line for at least 4 months, after which time we planned to rededicate the plant to other products which this customer could not use. This was an inordinately large line compared to where we had historically been. So, my mission and timeline were clear. Would the customer remain solvent for four more months, and would any potential losses exceed what we stood to generate in the way of profits? That second item represented a major question mark, since $350,000 represented a high water mark for us and a bad debt would wipe out a lot of income. In fact, a $350,000 loss would wipe out approximately one and a half year's profit on the account. The rewards were clear: the expected profits, and keeping the plant running and retaining our workforce which we could then easily shift over to the new product line.

One Wednesday morning, I got up at 4AM and traveled to the customer's offices to meet with their CFO and "temporary" controller (interpret: consultant). After a short discussion, they placed in front of me, in confidence, a *very* discouraging set of numbers. Numbers which, by themselves, would probably never compel anyone to extend credit. At that point, the consultant told me he had worked for a financially distressed customer years ago, and that he had worked with our existing management at the time to keep us as a supplier and keep us from taking a loss. I had no way of checking this story, as all our participants had long since retired. I simply believed the story to be true, and I found both gentlemen to be very trustworthy as we discussed how they planned to turn things around. Their plans seemed reasonable. Then, I looked them in the eye and asked the ultimate question: was bankruptcy a possibility? They assured me that it was not, and they assured me that we would not take a loss. Of course, these are promises that we hear every day, and deciding when to and when not to accept this promise is obviously the ultimate "test of our mettle." In this case, I accepted the promise, and I agreed to extend the line. In so doing, I realized that I was making a decision that, in general, ran counter to what other suppliers were independently doing. Most seemed to be continuing to draw down exposures in reaction to the earlier news releases, which contained numbers not nearly as negative as the newer figures I had just seen. And, most other suppliers had *not* made the personal visit.

In the ensuing four months, we shipped $1.3MM to

the account. We were paid right on time for every shipment. Our plant operated efficiently, and the changeover occurred smoothly. We were paid in full. The customer survived; successfully made the changes they planned, and returned to health without filing bankruptcy or making any kind of compromise with creditors. To my knowledge, through it all, they paid every trade bill on time.

For a time, these two men remained in the employment of this customer, and they used me as a credit reference on many occasions. They ultimately moved to other positions, at which time they began to use me as a personal reference.

Certainly, not every time we are promised "you won't get hurt" will be a credible promise. Making that decision correctly is our mission. Professionally, there is very little if anything that is more fulfilling than to "make this call" correctly, the rewards being profits, continued employment for our people, and sometimes lifetime relationships.

The story was awarded the prize for the best decision for a mid-sized company.

The Scriptural View

The scriptures are well directed in their admonitions about "trusting in man" as opposed to trusting in the Lord. To be sure, in my profession, I have been promised on many occasions that I would take no loss if I trusted and extended credit. I haven't been keeping a running total for the last 30 years, but certainly a fair amount of those promises were false.

Nonetheless, we obviously must have some basis for "trusting each other," even if unable to "trust *in* each other." We place our trust *in the Lord* and use the knowledge we gain from His counsel to decide when to trust each other.

In the world of business credit, trust is a crucial principle in many respects, not only in the trusting of the customer himself. When reference information is exchanged between credit professionals, the person receiving a reference on behalf of his company must not divulge, to the customer being discussed, the information that was provided by the reference giver. (This principal of *confidentiality*, a form of trust, diverges noticeably from the consumer credit world where generally the individual has broader rights to the exchanged information.) Also, reference givers are bound by a general unwritten code of conduct, based on honesty. For example, while a reference giver might be disinclined to freely share positive references, for fear of losing good business to competitors, such behavior would be unacceptable. Why would it be "unacceptable"?

In answering that question, the interesting thing is that there are not very many actual Federal or state laws to guide reference givers. While preparing a seminar that I conduct on business ethics, involving the exchange of credit references, I found only two actual written laws on the subject. So, what binds the profession in this understood code of conduct?

Unlike Ms. Katie Kite, whose story appears later in this book, I have never surveyed the entirety of my peers to ascertain the proportion who believe in Jesus. Rather, I must make an inference, based on (a) my knowledge that those who I know closely are indeed practicing Christians and (b) an interesting graph from Ben Cooper's "The Case for Theocentric Social Action"[34] which appears below:

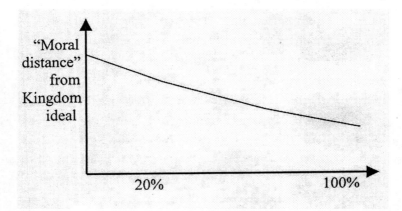

It is my belief that my peers and I have established our unwritten code of conduct according to the principles of Jesus' teaching. I see this in the fairness and honesty we impart to the sharing of information, and the way we deal with each other in other business matters as well. In the professional fraternity of business credit, those who act otherwise quickly find themselves ineffective and move out of the field.

Note that, at its right edge, Ben's theory encompasses what we know about our human imperfections. Even in a society which is truly 100% Christian, we fall far short of God's "Kingdom ideal," which would essentially be a society executing God's plan to perfection.

MEDIA NARANJA

David and Katrina were getting serious about getting married. (Actually, as Trina knew, Dave had purchased a ring but had not yet gained enough courage to present it to her!) Unfortunately, they had already been subjected to an enormous amount of advice on the topic, including an intimidating amount of statistics on how long it should take for this or that development. Trina became particularly frightened that the relationship wasn't proceeding "by the book." They were both quite torn about what they were hearing from their friends.

To put their situation in context, you must first understand the environment in which they (and I) operated. We were part of a huge church "singles" class comprised of people aged 28 to 60. Collectively we defined everything the word "single" could encompass: never married, divorced once, divorced several times, remarried to their original partner and then divorced again, trying new relationships, swearing off relationships, and so on. The membership of the group also "turned itself over" regularly, with people coming in, going out, back in again.35 The viewpoints to which this couple was exposed were similarly diverse. They were contemplating a long engagement relative to the courtship period, so their time of "trial" was going to be lengthy.

In the midst of this struggle, they approached me for

some advice. Before speaking to them, I thought for a day or so about what I should say, or if indeed I should say anything. I prayed, and then I received a visitation of the Holy Spirit who delivered ideas to my head in a rush. What I shared with them appears below:

NEVER:
1) Let friends decide for you how you feel about each other. There will be times when you think you just HAVE to let someone else know when your partner has hurt you. And, indeed, you may have to do that. But a true friend will listen and direct you right back to your partner to talk it out. The friend will not say "Oh, he or she is just not right for you" or anything like that, at least until such a thing has *long* become obvious to you too. Beware of acquaintances who may be jealous of losing their time with you.
2) Let "the crowd" tear away at your relationship. This can happen in very subtle unsuspecting ways. While you don't want to abandon your friends, pick and choose the time you spend with them and dedicate the real quality time to each other. I saw a very good marriage fail because the young partners did not plan a family (or at least a life for two) and instead spent more time with their friends than they did each other.
3) Let statistics RULE your life. You are not statistics; you are living, loving human beings. While this is not to say that you don't want to listen to good advice about pacing things, or other matters, don't question something that is going well just because you hear somewhere that it isn't supposed to be.

4) Fall into a "quasi-marital" relationship before you are married. Being together all the time in a way that simulates marriage is dangerous, especially during a long engagement.
5) Believe you must change each other. This isn't anything new; you've heard it before. You have to be ready to accept each other for who you are. I saw a funny video once about a husband who nagged his wife because she was always late, and by the time they got where they were going they were at each other's throats. After a few years, he just decided to accept it. As he said in the video, "We're still always late, but now we aren't mad anymore." One out of two isn't bad. Nagging tears at relationships.
6) Let your public expression of commitment stop you from making any changes in the relationship you feel you need to make. I've felt embarrassed many a time at what "people think of what I did" only to realize (in the circumstances at hand) it either wasn't that important or it really wasn't what they thought at all.

ALWAYS
1) Talk to each other, OPENLY. But don't think that failing to talk to each other every day, during the courtship, is bad. People who are right for each other are going to "be there" for each other even if they don't reaffirm their relationship every day. So, in fact, not talking every day is usually a better sign of confidence.
2) My wise friend A J Hewett once told a couple: "If you

each give *your share*, and *then a little more*, you'll make it."
3) Have a God-led marriage. Easy to say, but what does it mean? Does that mean just pray together and go to church a lot and so on? No, it means, to me, let the "right thing" be the barometer for your relationship. Most of the time, since we have a pretty common value set among us Christians, we will agree on what the right thing is. Even we crusty business folk agree on what the right thing is most of the time, even without laws to guide us. If failure to do the right thing hinges on the weakness of one partner to correct behavior patterns, resolve to make that correction. It may mean a correction for both people. Recognize that there may be an occasional time when you cannot agree on the right thing but those should be infrequent and rather inconsequential if you have a common spiritual center (see #5 above—how bad is it really to be late to most social functions?).
4) Agree to follow one learned human counselor, and the Counsel of the Almighty. I once went to a seminar where the speaker said:

"In the 70's, it wasn't '*what* you knew, it's *who* you knew'; in school it isn't '*what* you know, it's *when* you know it"; today it isn't 'who you *know*, it's who you *trust*.'"

BEWARE
1) Long engagements relative to the time of courtship can be *stressful by definition*. Doesn't mean change your plans if that's what you feel is best, but be aware you will both be under pressure as you look forward to

the happy event. Be patient with each other. It may be better to judge who the other person "really is" under different conditions than that. If you look at it as "Trial Period Part II," I *donnnnnn't think* that's what engagement is intended for!

2) Don't let the passages of long periods of time challenge your intimacy boundaries. And, one of the most intimate things in the world is praying together. Don't even do that until you are sure you're ready for your souls to be that close.

With God's Love and pulling for you,

Norm

The Scriptural View

The most appropriate scriptures involve, of course, the counsel of the Holy Trinity. For example, John 14:25-26, Jesus' words "All this I have spoken while still with you. But the Counselor, the Holy Spirit, whom the father will send in my name, will teach you all things, and will remind you of everything I have said to you." And First Kings 22:5 "But Jehoshaphat also said to the king of Israel 'First seek the counsel of the Lord.'"

The temptation to advise others is ever present in humans, so often without the advantage of having lived through that person's particular challenge. (A common admonition in the training of human counselors is to never say, "I know how you feel"!) There is only one Counselor who knows the walks of all shoes. When we fail to seek His leadership, we increase our chances of failure exponentially.

It is too soon to say if the advice will help produce a long happy marriage, but Dave and Trina are in their eighth month of a happy engagement. They have successfully separated themselves from the legions of advisors, have maintained their boundaries, and are still proceeding steadily toward the altar. What seemed most important at the time we talked is that they felt someone cared and listened, and took an unbiased positive approach with them. In fact, what I remember most is that they told me "So many people try to convince us we will fail." This may, of course, have been a function of jealousy spawned by frustrated members of the group who had failed in similar efforts at partnership. The Holy Spirit will never be constrained by such an emotion.

By the way, Dave is a silviculturist. A what? Someone who controls forest regeneration and growth and, in general, cares for trees. Hence his self-appointed nickname "Ranger Dave."

WHITNEY

As I cut the grass on our sloping front yard one hot summer day in 1990, I noticed a minivan pull up to our curb. A smiling mother hopped out of the vehicle, which was chock full of kids. I had, by the way, never met the lady, or any of the passengers. She pointed at my youngest daughter Whitney, sitting on the front steps, and enthusiastically asked, "Can *she* come with us?!"

This event, as much as anything, describes the personality Whitney developed as she grew. She quickly displayed strength for establishing strong friendships with other children, and for being a polite guest. Other parents regularly *asked us* if she could come over to visit their children.

Whitney is (a) like all the inhabitants of this book, not quite perfect, (b) beautiful, both inside and out, (c) a "regular teenager," at least at the time of this story. In other words, her dad admires her as any proud father would, but realistically recognizes that she has a little flaw or two.

My favorite symbol of her love is the "elephant" pencil holder she made for me: an empty soup can covered with construction paper, with a crinkled strip of a trunk and two scalloped ears glued on. On the day that she gave it to me, as I picked her up at kindergarten, she saw me far across the playground and yelled "Daddy!" A father standing next to me, who had obviously met her before in his visits to pick up his own child, smiled at me and said "I like that one."

The Thanksgiving holiday season of 2000 meant a plane trip to Cleveland, Ohio, to spend time with my mom and dad. My daughters, then both in high school, were looking forward to the quality time with their grandparents. Upon arriving, all faces were broad smiles as we waited on the luggage and kidded with each other. Whitney, to whom laughter comes easily (a friend of ours once said, "When she laughs her face just explodes"), was particularly enjoying herself. Bag after bag went by, the carousel stopped, and the smiles slowly disappeared as everyone realized Whitney's bag had never appeared. Whitney instantly and understandably turned into a teen who had lost all her important possessions, which probably requires no further explanation.

After a couple of unsuccessful tours around the carousel, we went to the baggage claims office, where she described her bag through the tears to the three people gathered there. The claims people were great; true sympathy flowed quickly, but of course did little to ease her pain. My mind turned to replacement, and I asked what she had lost that was most important to her.

Now, this was in my second year of divorce and, being the non-custodial parent, I was not accustomed to being so "distanced" from Whitney. I really had no idea what her response would be. The answer that I expected was along the lines of make-up, special sweater, etc.

The tearful words that struggled through her lips were among the most cherished, by me, that she ever spoke. The answer was "My Bible." No words can explain the love and warmth that flowed through me (and does so again as I type this), or the looks on the faces of the claims staff, her sister, and my parents. For some unknown reason, I guess my continued belief that there had to be something more "material" involved,

I asked "What else?" To which she replied "My book in which I write scriptures."

At that precise moment, I saw through the corner of my eye a baggage handler walking into the office with a familiar Hunter green sport bag in his hand. It had been left on the cart carrying the luggage from the plane to the baggage area. In seconds she was reunited with those things that, indeed, she could not have replaced for any sum of money. And, in that incredibly brief period of time, an unforgettable act of witness occurred.

Although I can conjecture about it, I can never know the impact of her witness on the airline employees. But I know the impact on me; it was the most moving act of witness I ever observed. The separation of the divorce process had, to that moment, kept me from knowing the strength of her faith. Even in marriage, it was not something that I think she could have simply told me about. I am convinced that God's Hand held her luggage aside, for those short minutes, for His Purpose. In so doing, He opened a door that perhaps could not have been opened by any other means.

The Scriptural View

Obviously Whitney's unprepared but inspired acts in the airport were a manifestation of the Great Commission. But, rather than looking to the abundant scriptures on witnessing, such as those quoted elsewhere in the Kevin Beckett and Katie Kite stories, let me turn to the quality of honesty. Certainly, Whitney's sudden expressions were an outpouring of the simple honesty of the feelings inside her, of her spirit laid bare. Consider Proverbs 12:17 (a) "A truthful witness gives honest testimony…" and 12:19 (a) "Truthful lips endure forever…" In its spontaneity, we would also consider Miriam's burst of song in Exodus 15:21 "Sing to the Lord for he is highly exalted..."

Jesus, in Mark 4:21-23 (NIV), spoke to the crowd, "Do you bring a lamp to put it under a bowl or a bed? Instead, don't you put it on its stand? For whatever is hidden is meant to be disclosed, and whatever is concealed is meant to be brought out into the open. If anyone has ears to hear, let him hear." And those in the airport claims office that day, indeed, had ears to hear.

KELLY

When the girls were small, the house where we lived was in the middle of the block. Therefore, it often became the gathering place for all the neighborhood kids, which I admit made me pretty happy. One particular day, I came home from work and noticed everyone was engaged in some kind of major drama, dressed up in this and that. When I inquired, the boy on all fours on the floor said, "Kelly told me to be the dog." The kid with the towel over his shoulders said (of course) "Kelly told me to be Superman."

One afternoon when I went to elementary school to pick up the girls, one of the teachers looked at me and shook her head. "We have an area that the kids are not supposed to run across," she explained. "Kelly dutifully walked across as always. Behind her, a little girl charged across after her. Kelly turned, put her hands on her hips, and said 'Jennifer, go back over there and walk across.' And the little girl did it."

Such was life with my oldest daughter. She seemed to have been born with a gift for directing and, as she grew, her assessment of other's skillsets grew well beyond how well they could imitate a dog. Her teachers would recognize this and assign her leadership roles in group projects. Her talent was accompanied by a bit of overconfidence at times, so we worked to help her balance her sense of self-security.

As she entered the third grade, I went to her orientation,

conducted by her teacher for the year ahead, Mrs. Wiseman. Mrs. Wiseman was clearly someone who commanded respect, and laid down a clear set of rules she expected the kids to follow. Up to this point in life, Kelly had never really had a strong teacher, and I worried about how she would respond. Which aspect of her personality would prevail: the dedication to rules displayed earlier, or the strong independent streak?

As time went on, I saw that the combination of teacher and student was perfect. This was the kind of leader Kelly had needed all along; firm, clear in her direction, no nonsense. Kelly and her best friend Melanie, our "back door" neighbor, clearly enjoyed the class and did very well.

It was during this time that something very special happened; Kelly wrote a short story that won a national award in the Knowledge Engineering Writing Contest. This is the story:

The Inch Long Alligator

Once a mother alligator laid her eggs near a swamp in some moss. They were all the same size except one. It was so small you could barely see it. When the eggs hatched, the mother was so proud. One of the babies was just an inch long and a half-inch wide. The mother named him Inchy. Inchy loved playing hide-and-peek (hide and peek is like hide and go seek). Inchy loved to play this game because he always won. One time Inchy rode on one of his brothers without him knowing it. It was time for the alligators to learn how to swim. Everyone caught on quickly but Inchy. So he didn't learn to swim.

The time came for the alligators to go out on their own, even Inchy. Inchy was scared. He knew that they had enemies, but he didn't know what they looked like. He met a friend named Alli. Alli taught him about storks, raccoons, and many creatures. The only thing he didn't know to teach Inchy about was a snake.

One day while they were walking, they met a snake. He looked friendly so they followed him. He sh...sh...showed them around his hole, but then he started to chase Inchy.

Inchy was cornered by the snake. The only way he could get away was by swimming. He closed his eyes and dived into the water. With his eyes closed he quickly swam to the other side of the swamp. When he opened his eyes, Inchy realized that he could swim. From that day on, he could do lots of other things and lived a happy scared free life.

By Kelly Taylor
Grade 3
Mrs. Wiseman's Class

OK, so I am proud of both my girls and worked them both in the book. And, yes, that by itself would be motive enough for me. But there is a lesson in that story, isn't there? The lesson is about overcoming one's fears (see page one). The hero did it because he "had to," but that's often the case isn't it? The important thing is, he did it.

Several years later, after we had moved to another city, the girls and I visited Melanie and her family. This was a new experience for all of us; it was the first time we had taken the girls back to their hometown. We visited the school and found Mrs. Wiseman, in the same room where she had taught before. Recognizing us, she beamed and gave Kelly a huge hug. "That class," she said, "was my best one ever. You, and Melanie, and the others, that class just crackled!"

The Scriptural View

Biblical parallels too numerous to mention abound on the subjects of courage and confidence inspired by God. For example, Daniel in the lion's den and, also in the book of Daniel, Shadrach Meshach and Abednego in the fiery furnace. The story of Esther, whose courage saved the Jewish people from destruction, is another.

For target scriptures on courage, let me suggest Psalms 27:14, 31:24, 37:3, and 37:28; Isaiah 40:29 and 43:1; 2 Kings 6:16; Philippians 4:12-13; and John 16:33.

Postscript

No false sense of pride would enable me to quote scripture as to my raising of these young ladies, or to say how my parenting embodied such spiritual words. I made many mistakes as a parent, but to talk about such goes well beyond the scope of this book. My own parents (see chapter *The Real Norman Taylor*) worked so hard making a living that, by necessity, they often were unable to spend the kind of time with me that they desired to. I determined to do as much with the kids as I could, while I could, before the teenage years (the YMCA Indian Princess program, painting the sanctuary of a small church south of Nashville, all kinds of work with the homeless). To that end, I succeeded, and later chapters will reveal to what end that effort bore fruit.

In one last (hopefully forgiven) burst of fatherly pride, I offer one of Kelly's poems:

GOD SPOKE AND HE SOUNDED LIKE....

Sand Castle Story

Long ago the ocean was still,
Calm, peaceful and quiet.
A young girl lived near on a hill,
And every day she'd walk by it.

One day the ocean called to her
From beneath its dark depths
"Come be our queen" it'd whisper
Until she'd finally accept.

She had one condition, though,
The ocean must bow before her.
The water began to toss and throw,
And the waves began tumbling over.

At this she was very pleased,
But still she wanted more.
"Roll me out a carpet," she teased,
As the waves crashed on shore.

The ocean began to create a foam,
Salty, thick and white.
On the waves to the shore it'd roam,
To the girl's delight.

Still she was not satisfied.
She wanted gifts of course!
To this request, the ocean replied:
"Starting with.....a horse?"

NORMAN TAYLOR

A seahorse, along with other gifts,
Washed onto the shore.
Through the sand, she'd dig and sift.
Finding gifts and shells galore.

Now the day was getting late,
And the sun beat down upon her.
She realized that on this huge estate,
There was no sort of shelter.

To the ocean she began to suggest
"I can't escape the sun with my hand."
And the ocean did its very best
To build a castle out of sand.

To this day the waves roll and crash,
The ocean still brings gifts
So maybe it wouldn't be to rash
To say that girl still exists.

-Kelly Taylor (1999)

SOUTH CAROLINA

For 36 years, I have driven the sunbaked roads of South Carolina in various pursuits. Each Friday during the summer of my 18th year, I wheeled a stoutly powered Chevy pickup out of its parking lot at Jordan Marsh Auto Parts, downtown Charlotte, NC, headed south down Highway 21. My mission was to deliver parts and supplies to the various garages and warehouses peppered along this main road and its arteries. For most weeks, the final delivery was Great Falls, SC. I took a left at the "T" intersection in town and then unloaded 40-pound bags of oil dry at a warehouse a mile or so down the road. Pretty tough duty for a 110-pound kid. Depending on who needed a special part or stock replenishment, I might veer as far west as Chester or perhaps even Saluda.

The personal challenge was to get back to the store in time to start enjoying my weekend. Failing at that, my predecessor quit the job. I ended the first trip by being back in the store parking lot at 3 minutes until 5PM. From the truck cab, I could see the owner through the window as he jumped up and ran to meet me. I expected hearty congratulations for a job well done. Instead, ignoring the empty truckbed, he glowered at me and said, "I thought we told you to deliver all those parts!" My "I did" sent him back to his office and the telephone. After several calls, he returned with a much calmer look on his face. One garage owner apparently told him, in jest, that I had driven by with the tailgate down, hit the brakes, his parts and his parts only flew off, and then I sped on to my next destination. In other words, I guess my predecessor's problem might have been too much socializing at each stop. Each successive Friday, my employers made it a little harder for me to accomplish my personal mission by adding more customers to the trip. You know the saying "No good deed goes unpunished" which, by the way, is NOT the lesson here.

There is a joke, passed on to me by a friend who moved here from Wisconsin. It asserts that there are signs at the state borders which say, "Welcome to South Carolina. Turn Your Clocks Back 30 years." Today, I drive these same roads, just in reverse, from the Southeast edges of South Carolina up to Charlotte and Greenville.36 Indeed, much of the state is pretty much the same today as it was when I was 18. For example, I recently bought a reproduction of a painting showing downtown Graniteville as it appeared in 1955. Except for the vintage of the cars in the scene, and one building (the old movie theater, now gone), the picture could have just as well been yesterday.

But much has changed and, in my view, not for the better. Interstate 77 bypasses the lengths of Highway 21 I used to drive. The roads are dotted with the ghosts of industries that are slipping from our countries' grasp, or are a shadow of what they once were. For example, the diminished presence of an apparel business like Knight Industries in Saluda, which recently closed its distribution center there. Just south of the town, a real estate sign ironically bearing the name "Southern Visions Realty" fronts a long empty warehouse.37 The bankrupt textile firm Martin Color-Fi, in Johnston, sits with tall untended patches of grass sticking through broken parking lot pavement. The giant textile company in Rock Hill, where many of my friends worked after we graduated from college, has been pieced up into diverse new foreign ownerships. These are just a few signs of the blight that can be seen throughout the state. Textile and related employment constituted approximately 15 % of state employment in the mid-1980's; today, it is less than 5%.

In 1972, a year and a half out of college, my roommate Bill and I moved from an apartment on the South side of Charlotte to a small house on Highway 160 near Fort Mill, SC. To the West of us was the Tega Cay resort community; to the East, the huge fabric manufacturer Springs Industries. To the north and south lay the cities of Charlotte and Rock Hill. Ultimately Jim and Tammy Bakker would settle into our area with their doomed Heritage USA religious compound. At the intersection of 160 and 21 sat a small roadside market known as "The Peach Stand;" your typical rough lumber structure with benches inside for display of the produce sold there. As for us, that little market pretty much represented our outlook; we lived in our own world, fairly oblivious to the big things a few miles distant.

The house was 100 years old and sat on a 120 acre wooded lot including an 8 acre lake. The owner's grandmother was born in the log cabin to the rear. The house had historical significance as having been owned by a Civil War veteran named Josiah Coltharp. There were 5 rooms, all having fireplaces except the kitchen, although in those days heat was provided by an oil furnace in the crawlspace. Bill and I had been joined there by Alfonso who, like Bill, was a Celanese engineer. Alfonso was 32, a Cuban immigrant, blessed with the best English vocabulary of anyone I knew. He was ten years older than Bill and I, and very much served as our "big brother."

In a couple of years, Bill and I had each married and moved on, and Alfonso had been hired by a major Midwestern firm which moved him to climes more Arctic than he could have imagined. I ultimately moved far from the Charlotte area, but every time I returned, I tried to visit "the Farm," as we had nicknamed the place. Over time, a gate was built to keep people from coming up the long driveway, and beer cans stacked up in the yard. I could only stand at the barricade and mourn both the decline and the isolation. Then, on the occasion of our 30th high school reunion, I turned into the drive, and the house was gone.

Thinking it demolished, I almost cried upon seeing Bill that evening at the reunion. (Bill had settled in Lancaster SC, and we no longer saw each other much except at the reunions.) A smile grew beneath his mustache, and he said "No! I was reading the local newspaper not long ago and saw a photo of a house being towed down a road. I thought it looked familiar. As I looked closer, I realized it was the place we had lived. Underneath, the story explained the house was to become the nature center of the Springs Close Greenway on Highway 21, two miles north of the Peach Stand intersection. Go over there in the morning!"

That Sunday morning, I followed Bill's directions. The Peach Stand had now become a nice modern minimarket complete with restaurant, various connoisseur items, and gas pumps, although the old now-shuttered structure still sat across the street. I turned onto the marked road running through a small section of cleared land, topped a small rise, and there in the light morning rain sat the house. For the first time in decades, I stepped onto the old wooden porch, under the filigreed adornments that transversed the posts and ceiling. Disappointed that no one seemed to be around to let me in, I held my breath and turned the doorknob. To my surprise, it opened.

At the time, I was reading a book on sacred places called

Jerusalem, One City Three Faiths by Karen Armstrong (1996, Ballantine Books, NY). Personally, having been away from my birthplace for some 45 years,38 I did not know much about personal sacred places. But, in a few minutes, I was about to understand quite a bit on the subject.

The very air inside the house was an energized living organism.39 Voices of the past, dear friends, couples who met there and later married, saturated me as I stood there. My old high school friend Roger Briggs, and his wife Beth, now in Guatemala with their Christian ministry "Hearts for Heaven," had seen their spirits grow together there, their love for each other and their God deepen. Jimmy and Alethea, Bill and Beth, so many more. And, indeed, the beginnings of my own marriage were there, a memory shaded by the later events but nonetheless still so powerful in the good things it did produce. But Someone else was there in the house too.

My old bedroom was the only locked area, now being the Ranger's office, a man named Billy Barron. It took several trips before I caught him there and was able to go in. He shared with me the story of the Greenway. Springs Industries, to protect the local history and their own traditions, had moved the house, and the log cabin, to land they had dedicated for the Greenway. The area is now used for hiking, for school trips in which children receive education on local history, wildlife and vegetation, and so on. Pictures of Josiah Coltharp dot the walls, and in Bill's old bedroom now live mounted remains of various local animals.40. I still go back there every chance I get.

Postscript

So what is the lesson here? In this story, there is no person or persons setting examples, no occasion of human tenderness or tough love. Rather, the lesson is that the Holy Spirit moves not only through people but through *places* as well. Those first moments in the house, there was no question that the loudest voice was God's, telling me how he had been there for the orchestration of those lives. How he had forged those bonds. How that, even in apparent failure, good fruits had been produced, children were born who would impact lives for the better, hearts for mission would grow. And He still resides in those hearts and people today. Sometimes, he just leads us to go back to these sacred places and remind ourselves of His Presence.

ANYWAY

This prayer is performed as a song on the compact disk "Zero Church" by Suzzy and Maggie Roche. They were told that it was written by Mother Teresa and inscribed on the wall of her orphanage in Calcutta. However, they were subsequently informed by Sister M. Nirmala M. C. at the Missionaries of Charity in Calcutta that this was not the case. Others said that the poem was found by Mother Teresa's bedside when she died, written in her own handwriting.

Anyway

People are often unreasonable, illogical and self-centered
Forgive them anyway
If you are kind, people may accuse you of selfish ulterior motives
Be kind anyway
If you are successful, you will win some false friends and some true enemies
Succeed anyway
If you are honest and frank, people may cheat you
Be honest and frank anyway
What you spend years building, someone could destroy overnight
Build anyway

If you find serenity and happiness, they may be jealous
Be happy anyway
The good you do today, people will often forget tomorrow
Do good anyway
Give the world the best you have, and it may never be enough
Give the world the best you've got anyway
You see, in the final analysis, it is between you and God
It was never between you and them anyway

-Author Unknown

While the source of "Anyway" remains mysterious, we do know that Mother Teresa spoke some of the most humbling words ever uttered, "We cannot do great deeds, only small deeds with great love."

"THE REAL NORMAN TAYLOR"

It would be hard to write text about life's lessons and leave out one's parents. The focus here, for reasons that will become clear as the story unfolds, is my dad. This is not intended to minimize in any way what I learned from my mom, who understands human motivations better than anyone I ever knew. Whatever perceptive powers I gained (including the yearning to see the good in others, which helped me to write this book) came mostly from mom. In terms of integrity and honesty, Nathanael had nothing on my mother.

By God's Plan, although it appeared to have been an accident, I followed in the career footsteps of my dad. When I was 12 years old, he took me aside and talked to me about the 25 or so men and women who worked for him. These individuals ran the credit and collections operations of retail stores in a two state area. They were seen as the "black hats" in the organization, the people who did the tough work. Dad wanted them to feel appreciated for their good work just like anyone else. He had given them all upbeat nicknames like "Flash" and took photos of them. He wanted to recognize the best five performers every month in the intercompany flyer. My job was to draw caricature pictures of them to accompany the stories he would write. My first business job.

My mom and dad had both followed a work ethic born of many influences; growing up in the depression, poor, in the small rural communities of Western Kentucky.41 Dad's circumstances left him with little formal education. They both had to work hard to provide for the family; dad often had jobs where he worked long hours and at night. This provided them little or no time to teach me sports or carpentry, to play games, or other things that engage direct teaching methods.

I can only remember one occasion, a very humorous one at that, when mom's perceptive abilities threw her a curve. My teenage friend Ronnie, who she had never met before, dropped by unexpectedly one day for lunch. Ronnie's appearance was always wild and unkempt. His clothes were wrinkled and his hair looked as though it had been combed with a propeller blade. He had a peculiar speech pattern which caused him to frequently interrupt his sentences with the expression "aaahhh." As I was washing up for the meal, mom burst into the bathroom with a wild wide-eyed expression on her own face. "Who is that person?" she asked. She continued to watch Ronnie suspiciously through the meal. Finished, Ronnie softly wiped his hands on the napkin, looked mom straight in the eye and said "Aaaahhh, Mrs. Taylor, that was the, aaahh, finest meal I ever ate. You are, aaahhh, a wonderful cook." A few minutes later, I ran into mom again, near the back of the house. Smiling broadly, she said "What a *nice* young man."

When I was 16, dad handed me the keys to the family car. There was a catch; every Saturday and two weeknights (Monday and Friday) I'd be driving across town to work in a retail tire store. The idea was that I would pump gas and that would be it (this was long before everyone in America discovered they could handle that just fine by themselves). At 110 pounds with rocks in my pockets, dad wasn't too keen about me changing tires on the pneumatic machines (which *haven't* changed much in the ensuing 35 years). However, feeling uncomfortable not carrying my share of the load with my co-workers, I learned to work the machines nonetheless. Ultimately I tried to get my hands on every tough assignment that came in the door.

Although I know I somewhat resented not being out with my friends at Friday night ballgames and Saturday trips, I didn't have much social life anyway. By day, I was top ten academically in a large high school class, and the all-time consummate "nerd." By night, I now worked with some of the roughest characters around. I came to appreciate that, by putting me to work in this environment, dad had given me several gifts. First, he taught me that hard work wouldn't hurt me. Secondly, the job put me in the company of all kinds of "worldly" folks, which helped me balance out the absence of such in my school life. (Jocks don't associate much with nerds, of course.) This second gift was dad's way of bestowing on me his special talent of being able to get along with anybody of any age or ethnicity. The term "never met a stranger" was written for dad. This also toughened me emotionally; the third gift being it toughened me physically as well.

Not long ago, the talk among the seven men in our Bible Study turned to our relationships with our fathers. I was surprised to find that only two of us (one of which was me) had positive images of our dads. As we shared our experiences, I remembered that I never faulted dad for the many things he couldn't teach me. I understood the reasons why. And I also had *the great exception.*

When I was 21, on my first job after college, the credit manager in the store where I worked was let go. The boss asked, "Does anybody know anything about this job?" "Yes sir, I drew pictures of credit people when I was 12." "It's yours." That spawned the great exception. At the time, I was living at home, and every night when I came home, dad asked me what challenges I faced and what I did. On almost every occasion, he encouraged me that I was "great," and sometimes sprinkled in some suggestions. It was perhaps his first real chance to teach me directly, and he taught me well. Those were the closest times we had together, relationally and geographically, as soon we would be separated by a distance of over 500 miles. Today, that geographic separation is even greater.

As I grew in the profession, I began to write articles for business magazines. Since dad and I share a name (one Sr., one Jr.) his friends would always congratulate him on his nice article. He would always respond "Oh no, that's written by the *real Norman Taylor*. (That taught me another lesson: humility.)

One day a dear friend was kind enough to publish something for me. I knew dad would want a copy, so I asked the friend to send him one with a cover letter. The cover letter was addressed to "The Best Credit Manager in the World" from the "Real Norman Taylor." And, yes dad, you are the best dad too.

Postscript

In terms of motivation of others, dad taught me many lessons. There aren't many business challenges tougher than a credit manager learning how to get along well with the sales department. The credit people are generally considered to be corporate overhead, necessary evils, and sometimes even jokingly referred to as the "sales prevention" department.

As I proceeded in the profession, I had my share of troubles, as chronicled earlier (see the *Luke* chapter). But, like the inch long alligator, to survive I ultimately had to grow, hard headed as I was. One technique that I ultimately adopted was to recognize the sales professionals for special things they did to help the credit department, information about accounts that helped us make better decisions, helping us collect money, and so forth. My platform for this was the annual sales meeting where I was allotted a short presentation in some unobtrusive time slot. My recognition tool of choice was a baseball cap from the college of the salesman to be awarded. The recognition was given in surprise form, with no advance notice prior to the presentation.

In the beginning, I didn't have many believers that sales people and a stubborn credit person could happily co-exist. My first award was, by design, to Dan, a salesman with whom I had had some pretty major battles. As I walked to his seat and laid the hat beside him on the table, he turned to the man next to him and said, "Here, you take the ___ hat. I don't want it." I carried on with the rest of my presentation as best I could. As I stood at the back of the room at the end of the meeting, I felt a hand lightly touch my shoulder. I turned around to find Dan; the hat perched firmly on his head. He reached out his hand to mine and said "Thank you."

Over time, as business got worse and the sales presentations themselves became less optimistic, the little "awarding of the hats" became a bright spot to which everybody looked forward. In one incredible act of God, as I watched the sports scores one Sunday afternoon, I noticed that the schools of the two "award recipients-to-be" had played a football game against each other over the weekend. Now, for some schools, this is hardly unusual, but this wasn't exactly "University of Miami—Florida State" or "Florida-Georgia" or "Michigan-Notre Dame." Although I'm a pretty avid sports fan, I didn't know either of these schools even had football teams, and neither had I ever known them to play each other at any sport. Fortunately for me the recipients weren't sensitive about this fact, so we all had a good laugh about it at the meeting.

Reconciliation is often a pretty tough thing for us humans. Pride gets in the way. When I think of what happened between Dan and me, I think about Matthew 5:23-24 "Therefore, if you are offering your gift at the altar and there remember that your brother has something against you, leave your gift there in front of the altar. First go and be reconciled to your brother, then come and offer your gift." Surely I would have gotten a better initial reaction from Dan had I heeded those words and been reconciled to him before I tried to give him the gift of praise. But at least achieving reconciliation in that moment paved the way for later application of the verse. Of course, I was also grateful for Dan's grace in humbling his pride, which made it all possible.

One final word about my parents. A popular TV talk show recently aired an episode featuring "romantic men." My mother, believing the show's producers had missed the point as to what constituted true male romanticism, wrote the following letter:

Dear Oprah:

As a long time fan of your show, I recently watched the episode on "romantic men" with particular interest. I couldn't help but think that "romanticism" defines itself in more ways than flowers, the candle-lit dinner, and a sumptuous meal prepared by a man.

Let me share with you my own most loving and kind man. I think you will find, in this story, the flower of a romanticism grown from deeper roots; roots of determination, grit, and self-giving.

GOD SPOKE AND HE SOUNDED LIKE....

My husband's name is Norman Taylor, Sr. He, along with his then-pregnant mother, was abandoned by his father when Norman was one year old. The date and place was the rural American Midwest of the early 1930's, a time of deep depression throughout the land.

Norman's father "went to the city to look for work," leaving the family with Norm's maternal grandparents. He never came back, and efforts to locate him proved fruitless. The grandparents were poor tenant farmers with 5 other children at home. Norm's mother ultimately miscarried the child who would have been his sibling. She herself then died young (27 years old), of pneumonia, when he was 7. He continued to live with his dear grandparents who taught him to be a man.

The father married again and adopted a little girl. He did not support them either. We do not know what happened but the wife and child were soon out of the picture. He eventually was married four times.

But this is not a story of those failures. Rather, it is a story of how one model of failure was overcome by one memorable life. As a consequence of the lack or parental support, times were hard, and our lives have never been easy. Educational opportunities had to take a back seat to the necessity of working for a living at an early age. My husband has worked very hard, unrelentingly, for decades to support me and our two sons. When the children were 5 and 3, we moved to rough and tumble East St. Louis, where he worked the night shift for a chemical company. Having no car, he waited on freezing streetcorners for his daily ride to work.

Our first home there was a house shared with another family. We occupied two rooms; the kids shared an army cot as a bed. Ultimately, his hard work provided an opportunity in business management, where his qualities began to shine. In 1989, he retired after 29 years of productive employment for Bridgestone-Firestone as a credit manager.

Although these professional achievements required considerably more than a "40 hour work week," Norman's heart for charity still led him to carve out enormous chunks of time for others. Wherever we have lived, our friends and neighbors have benefited from his service in ways almost too numerous to mention: shoveling snow from driveways, carrying clothing to dry cleaners, home repairs, etc.

The acts of service include all manner of work in the various churches where we have worshiped: finance committees, grass cutting, managing a team of men to build a picnic pavilion.

Today, at the age of 76, he serves on a ministry which provides transportation for convalescents. He also takes disabled men to lunch once a month.

In closing, let me respectfully ask you to consider this example of "another kind of romanticism" for inclusion in a future show. I think that this story is well worth sharing with your viewers.

Patty Taylor

Unfortunately, we heard nothing further. But maybe in a future show.....!!!

PHIL WASHER

When divorce became unavoidable, I signed up for a workshop in which Phil was one of the facilitators. In fact, I signed up for quite a few counseling sessions, and ultimately I seemed to overload myself with counsel. After a time, confused, I went to Phil and asked him to help me identify the most important factors to seek out, or to avoid, if I was ever to be qualified for another marriage. Brevity and accuracy being definite spiritual gifts for Phil, he provided me with a few simple terms and phrases that I don't believe I can ever forget.

"Healing While in a Relationship"—the name of the fictitious book Phil said he planned to write someday. The moral: deal with your own issues before you open yourself to partnership with a significant other.

"Two ticks, no dog." So many times, two people are drawn together almost entirely by the belief that one party can help fulfill the other's selfish personal needs. Both people are very needy ("ticks") and neither is healthy enough to provide nourishment ("the dog"). For a time, they can only see that they are similarly wounded, and believe that providing mutual comfort for their wounds will be all they need to flourish in relationship. They are victims of the aforementioned fable about healing. The nourishment for the relationship is missing, and the needed nourishment might come in all kinds of forms depending on the situation: mutual faith in God (most important), financial stability, emotional health, and so on.42

"Common spiritual foundation"—the most important thing to identify in a potential partner is to be equally yoked in a spiritual foundation that is consistent with your own.

"So you don't like the cards you've been dealt. Well, let's play them anyway." The advice a physician (one who worked to treat Phil as a whole, both in body and spirit) gave Phil shortly after he lost his job within three weeks of learning of his own impending divorce. The message was to make the most out of whatever circumstances we encounter.

"Chasing the Holy Grail of Enoughness"—the fallacy of following the common myth that, oh, if you'd just done a little bit more you could have avoided divorce, or similar bad fate.

"It isn't illegal to be single." Self explanatory!

THE LONG TEN FEET

I can never forget the title of an article I saw years ago: "Public Speaking and Other Coronary Threats." Surveys indeed show that, for many, speaking in public is a fear rivaled only by fear of death. The following is a "re-write" of an article of mine, which was published by *Business Credit* magazine in 1993. A few days after it appeared, a friend called to tell me that he had shown it to his daughter, and it helped her get through a tough presentation that she had to make. The simple knowledge that this article helped *one* young lady overcome that kind of fear made me feel very good. I hope that, by its appearance here, this piece may help many others.

Way up on the front row, you are seated next to a friend, talking nervously with them and trying to act as cool as possible. At the back of your brain, a sledgehammer of dread is beating rhythmically on an anvil of worry. The room suddenly erupts in a flurry of applause. Ten feet away, the speaker on the stage nods proudly in appreciation and says, "Now we welcome our next speaker….."

You force a smile and rise from your chair. Your head feels like someone has taken a bicycle pump and filled it with air, pushing out every intelligent thought. Your peripheral vision goes black, your legs are jelly, and an invisible person has you by the throat. You wobble toward the stage, a lake of saliva growing under your tongue. You move behind the podium with the grace of a wounded gazelle, open your mouth and say.........

Sound familiar? It's amazing that even people who seem to speak in public with the greatest of ease say they experience this same thing. For the first 42 years of my life, I went through this, or worse, every time I was called upon to make a presentation. Unfortunately, the few talks that I was forced into were usually work-related affairs in front of a bunch of sales people who didn't much like the latest round of credit decisions. That didn't help much.

In 1991, my (then) employer sent me to New York City to a seminar conducted by a prominent management association. Upon arriving, I was informed that our group was "lucky," we were going to have their "best instructor." I was pretty sure I knew what that meant; that I was about to meet the most intimidating, heartless human being I had ever seen. I was right. The stern lady that entered the room gave us five minutes to prepare a five-minute biographical speech, which was to include our comments as to what we expected to get out of the class. The first speaker, dressed in a perfectly fitting three piece suit, explained to the smooth choreography of his hand movements that he was a young executive vice president seeking to improve his "poor" speaking skills. The second presenter was a young lady in the armed forces absolutely brimming with self-confidence, which brought a huge smile to our instructor's face. On and on it went until I thought, "*Why* in the world are *these people* here?" Then came my turn and, well, never mind what happened. I was made even more self-conscious than usual by the fact that I was the only person there with a good old Southern drawl.

This went on for two days, during which time I struggled

to find any place to hide, any way to make the time speed by, any kind of relief. Finally, late in the second day, the instructor told us "When you speak to people, imagine that you are giving them a gift."43 My ears perked up. I liked that. Being a giver was particularly appealing to me.

A little later, she asked me "What's the matter, don't you Southerners ever tell stories? You are ordered to put at least four stories in your next assignment here." On the third day, I did that, and I was amazed at the results.

Those few words that she said changed my life. I had something to grab onto, something to take my focus away from the simple act of having to speak. I soon volunteered to do something relatively unthreatening; I taught a weekly, two and a half hour professional class to my peers in other companies. Knowing them and their companies well, I tried to salt every presentation with something that I knew would benefit them and maybe even make them look good to their bosses. I loaded my talks with past experiences, the tons of interesting stories that I found in that history. From that step, I grew stronger with each new opportunity, and I stress the word "opportunity," as that's how I began to see it.

Did I stop being nervous? No, as I said above, virtually everyone seems to say they never get past that, and I am no exception. I suppose the adrenaline rush to run from the tiger is a natural chemical reaction. The key is to use some device, such as the "gift" idea, to turn this nervousness into the excitement about what you are about to convey.

When someone tries to fix their golf swing, or their bowling approach, they will sometimes overload themselves with too much advice, or try to straighten out too many things at once. To prevent that, what I've tried to do below is offer just a few suggestions as to how you might tackle this monster.

- *Establish a Joyful Personal Purpose for Speaking.* Find the one thing that takes your mind off speaking itself; that translates it into something you enjoy. For me, it was the gift idea, for you, it may be something else. It could be cooking metaphors for topics unrelated to cooking, or maybe sports metaphors, and so on.44
- *Solid Openers.* Come up with something that gets their attention at the start. The first few minutes are crucial, to bring the audience in and to get yourself comfortable as well.45 Now, don't get confused as to what this opener should be. It doesn't have to be a joke or anything very dramatic. I started one speech, to the sales department, with the words (spoken softly) "How would you like to get *every* new account approved for credit?" Of course, this was impossible, but they were all ears. Then I spoke to them about how they needed to get credit applications filled out properly by prospective customers.
- *Stories.* Tell them. You might think you don't have any interesting ones, but I bet you do.
- *Prepare.* There is no substitute for that. Knowing you are prepared will help make you comfortable. Avoid overconfidence when presenting familiar material. If you are dusting off an old presentation, put some new things in it to make it fresh. Otherwise you will probably look just as stale as the material.
- *Volunteer.* As mentioned above, take the opportunities to get in front of others. Make yourself. Start with something in which the audience is sympathetic. Churches and professional organizations are great for this. Teach a Sunday School class.

The Scriptural View

I came across Brian Banashak's *Little Book of Business Wisdom* on the shelves at a bookstore in the Atlanta airport. At first, I was jealous; so much of what he writes is similar to the message I was ever so slowly trying to finish and convey in these pages. His opening acknowledgment, for example, gives thanks to friends and mentors for their lessons. But envy quickly gave way to appreciation. His weaving of Bible verses to business principles is thoughtful and succinct; a beautiful testimonial to the idea that a businessperson can indeed incorporate Jesus into business practices, and will in fact flourish by doing so.

At the very end, page 88, Brian offers the advice "Hang in there baby—it's not over til it's over." His Bible verse of reference is 2 Timothy 4:7, "I have fought the good fight, I have finished the race, I have kept the faith." We might also visit Romans 5:3 (b)-5, "…we know that suffering produces perseverance; perseverance, character, and character, hope. And hope does not disappoint us, because God has poured out his love into our hearts by the Holy Spirit whom he has given to us."

And, to all who would shun the opportunity of public speech, I would offer Matthew 5:14-16, "You are the light of the world. A city on a hill cannot be hidden. Neither do people light a lamp and put it under a bowl. Instead they put it on its stand, and it gives light to everyone in the house. In the same way, let your light shine before men, that they may see your good deeds and praise your Father in heaven."

I mentioned that, for me, the idea of giving a gift was the key that helped me overcome my fear. As Christians, what greater gift do we have to give to others than the joy of knowing

Jesus Christ as Savior and Lord? To be sure, the fear of offering our inner selves before others, as though naked, is a great and true fear. (And I pause here to break the counseling rule— I *do* know how you feel!) However, it is a fear which can be overcome through prayer and a personal relationship with God. When that happens, you will find some of the most enjoyable visitations of the Holy Spirit that you ever experienced. Trust me, and trust *in* God, on that assurance.

CHARLIE MISSROON

If any person taught me the true meaning of responsibility for those under your direction, it was Charlie Missroon. Before I had the good fortune to come under Charlie's wing, I had mostly worked for, well, some pretty weak leaders. One fateful day, he walked down to my office and informed me I would be joining the group of managers under his domain. I realized that this was being done for my good, to direct me on to a better path.

Charlie's ideas about managing others included a sincere desire to see them grow both as employees and *individuals*. Without a doubt, he believed that getting the work done, and done right, came first. However, he also felt that his role in the workplace was to provide opportunities for personal maturation and career development. With every misstep, he counseled me, which helped satisfy the part about getting the job done right. On the second front, he convinced me that I needed to do something for myself outside of the office. This led me to enroll, at the age of 31, in the Masters of Business Administration evening program at a local college. Five years later, I completed the objective and, in the ensuing 20 years, I have found how indispensable that degree has been to my professional growth.

One day, by accident, I made a surprising discovery. I found out that Charlie himself had never graduated from college. That only made his encouragement all the more special to me, since I realized he could simply have sunk into bitterness about how that had held him back professionally. All of us who worked for him felt he had been overlooked for many deserved promotions, without knowing how the education issue might have played into the decisions of upper management. We simply admired how he accepted the results and drove on.

Charlie was also unafraid to be friends with his subordinates, comfortable that his own strength of character permitted that kind of closeness. One particular afternoon, as we talked idly in his office (a common "bonding" event), he asked me a strange question: "Do you know how many bricks are in a square foot?" Now, since we were in the apparel business, not construction, I was a little mystified why he would inquire about such a thing. To my "no," he replied "six and a half." To my "Why would you need to know that?" he said "So you'll know if your contractor is hauling any bricks off on you." I stayed mystified until his later announcement that he was leaving the company to start his own construction company with his sons.

His "going away" party was an event of mixed feelings for me. Despite my then shyness of being in front of people, I wasn't about to let anyone else function as host. One of his going away presents was a puzzle I made. You got it; it was square drawn on a piece of white poster board, the measurements being a foot on each side. The puzzle pieces were six, and one half, bricks.

The Scriptural View

"The difference between courage and discourage rests in the presence or absence of encourage" (Life Truths Learner Guide, Spring 2004, Lifeway Church Resources)

Biblical parallels for Charlie's encouraging character

abound in Paul and Barnabas. Barnabas was an early convert of the apostle's teachings. He is introduced in Acts 4:36 "Joseph, a Levite from Cyprus, whom the apostles called Barnabas (which means the Son of Encouragement) sold a field he owned and brought the money and put it at the apostle's feet." Throughout the latter part of Acts, he accompanies Paul in his missionary journeys.46

Paul's letters to the various churches, in books such as Colossians and Thessalonians, are filled with reassurance. In 1 Thessalonians, we have many verses of support for Christians in need: 3:2, referring to Timothy's mission to Thessalonica to encourage the infant church; 4:18 "Therefore encourage each other with these words"; 5:11 "Therefore encourage one another and build each other up, just as in fact you are doing"; and 5:14 "And we urge you, brothers, to warn those who are idle, encourage the timid, help the weak, be patient with everyone."

During my time with the Planters Peanut-Lifesavers division of Nabisco, I was exposed to some of the best motivational experiences that I ever had the pleasure of experiencing. It reminded me of Charlie's personal work in encouraging me, carried out to the level of corporate execution. The particular device, which was most memorable to me, was the ACE award, although it is now lost on me exactly what that acronym meant. The idea was this: every month, associates were nominated to receive an award for their extraordinary achievements during the period. A committee reviewed the written nominations and chose a winner. (Eloquence on the part of the nominator didn't hurt in getting one's candidate chosen, I found.)

Experience taught us that it should be the clerical staff, rather than the managers, who received most of the awards, as this had the best impact on corporate morale. That said, the particular monthly award I remember most had nothing to do with the winner (a clerical associate), but rather with a fellow manager who had been nominated. Joe was a customer service manager, a burly rough and tumble Pennsylvanian, transplanted to North Carolina in the days approaching his retirement from the company. Endowed with the perhaps odd combination of technical brilliance and coal mining upbringing, Joe was, for me, a constant source of relief from the corporate rat race. Joe wasn't a fan of the award; he basically thought it was a bunch of fluff and baloney (he used somewhat stronger negative terms). At least, that was his opinion until the day he was nominated. During the award meeting, he sat next to me, giggling with glee, until the winner was named, at which point his lower lip could have been used as a diving board. After that, I never heard much from him about the process, pro or con.

As mentioned at the beginning, the purpose of these stories is to uplift, but the counterpoint of bad management techniques deserves some *small* pace for admonition. Indeed, I had some experiences that seemingly served only to demonstrate practices to avoid. For example, the company whose version of the ACE award meant black tie dinners for the upper management, who ceremoniously nominated themselves year after year. All you had to do was walk in the office any day, look at the expression on a clerical employee's face, and you could see the impact of this approach to management.

MARY DUNCAN, MOTHER

Dr. Wendell Duncan is a fellow congregant at Warren Baptist, a surgeon by profession. Physically trim, neat, diminutive in stature (5' 6"), with an ever-resent smile on his face. What is most visible in Wendell, though, is the missionary's heart, perhaps especially for the underprivileged. As a lay leader, he chairs our Community Ministry Council and is active in many other committees. He is a regular participant in the Ecuador and other medical missions.

Early in our friendship, I asked him the source of his zeal. To which he quickly answered "My mother Mary." That conversation led to this testimonial which I asked him to contribute:

August 7, 2003

Dear Norm,

As promised, I'm writing about the ministry of my Mom's life and what an impact her servant's attitude had on so many. At the age of 68, earlier this year, Mary E. Duncan went Home to be with Jesus and her funeral was a celebration of her life in Christ and a worship and praise experience the likes of which I've never encountered at someone's death. If she could speak to us I'm sure she would say that she didn't die, she just took her worship to a higher plane. In the intensive care unit before her death, her nurse said, "your mom must be proud to have a son who's a doctor." To which I replied, "What she is proud of is having 4 sons who all love the Lord, and are involved in missions and ministries." You see, my brothers and I had an awesome mentor.

Mary Duncan was very humble and full of humility and wouldn't want me talking about her many accomplishments, but I can't help but share of how she touched thousands with the love of Christ...not only through service but through her beautiful singing voice. She had many hardships in life. As a child her father died and she had to spend part of her youth in an orphanage when her mother couldn't take care of 3 children. Later she developed a loving relationship with a stepfather that lasted across many miles, until her death. She was valedictorian of her high school class, but married young and soon had 4 boys, so she didn't go on to higher education (until later in life). Mom was a tireless church worker and during part of my childhood she served at a small mission church in the farmlands outside of Chattanooga. There, I experienced the Great Commission first hand. Sadly, her marriage failed after 16 years, yet the Lord used her single-again status (as He did in the Apostle Paul's life) to give her the time and energy to minister throughout the rest of her life. Chronic obesity was another hardship and the complications thereof took her life prematurely, but she never let that slow her desire to minister to the "least of these my brothers", even when she was in a wheelchair. She was known as a big woman with an even bigger heart.

My own calling to community ministries began at a young age when Mom would take her 4 sons with her to the Atlanta Rescue Mission and minister to the homeless men through her beautiful voice and through serving in the soup kitchen. It was many years later before I would realize how the Lord would use those Friday nights to mold the ministries of 4 young boys who, at the time, would have much rather been at a ball game.

Despite having to often work 2 jobs to support her family, Mom also volunteered in the late '60's at the Atlanta 14th street "Hippie Clinic" and at the "Baby Clinic" for indigent mothers. There I received my introduction to medicine and the Lord used those early experiences to give me a heart, years later, for short-term medical missions. Only God knows how many lost, drug-scarred, and pregnant young people were touched at those clinics by Mary Duncan's love for Christ.

As she aged and her health failed further, her ministry was more church based. Her hunger for knowledge and her renown as a Bible teacher grew at about the same pace as her library of religious writings. Even in her 60's she took seminary classes to obtain a Bible teaching degree and her pastor, Dr. Gary Christiansen, spoke of her as a lay-pastor. Besides serving on most every committee at Christ the King Lutheran Church in Atlanta, she founded a ministry that took communion to the shut-ins and hospitalized. She was a faithful giver to numerous charities, yet often with funds that she needed to pay her bills. She knew that the Lord would provide. She was a tireless encourager and inspiration to many young pastors and other believers, but especially to her 4 sons, 3 daughter-in-laws, and 6 grandchildren.

Frequently while chairing a Community Ministries Council meeting, I think of that big woman with a heart the size of her home state of Texas, soothing those homeless men with her angelic voice as they waited for a hot meal and a place to sleep.

J. Wendell Duncan, MD

Postscript

Reading this, I regret that I never had the pleasure of *meeting* Mary Duncan, but I was enabled to *know her* through this story and her reflection in her son. And, it has to bring a smile to read his description of her as a physically large person, to compare that image to Wendell's slight physical presence, and then realize that their hearts were probably exactly the same size. As big as Texas.

HEARTS FOR HEAVEN

As fellow junior high school students in Charlotte, North Carolina, in 1963, Roger Briggs and I could not possibly have foreseen how our lives would become intertwined.47 Roger and his future wife Beth had many of their early dates in the house where I lived after college (see chapter *South Carolina*); shortly after, he was a groomsman in my own wedding. As a young dentist, he took an assignment to a remote mountain community (Hayesville, North Carolina), as part of a program designed to place medical personnel in underserved areas. Later, Roger and Beth and their young family became involved in medical mission visits to Guatemala, one month each year. The Lord ultimately called them to move to the country and build a ministry they appropriately named "Hearts for Heaven."

The year of 2001 brought, to my life, the start of a series of business trips to Guatemala. Having kept up with Roger and Beth sporadically by mail over the years, I soon became enchanted with the idea of catching up with them, although I wasn't sure if we could logistically work it out. Shortly before my third trip, I was delighted to find they would be able to pick me up at the airport, and that we would be able to share dinner in Zone 10 in Guatemala City. 48

As we talked, together for the first time in 15 years, I remembered something Roger had told me when we were teenagers. Actually, it was a question he asked me: "Do you want to help people?" Neither of us can remember why he asked that, but two things are definitely true. First, it was a simple expression of Roger's own deep desires, ultimately fulfilled in a huge way. Secondly, those few words made a very big impression on my (as yet unformed) servant heart.

I recently asked Beth to write down their story, in her own way. I knew she was *very* busy, so I was not surprised when she asked for some additional time to reflect and do that. Then, about 24 hours later, I received the following e-mail from her. It's amazing how God opens us up when he fills us with the Holy Spirit.

"It will take me some time to write down history; spiritual highlights and description of where we are today. It has certainly been a fascinating life. If I were to outline our life I would list the highlights as:

1949 the year that each of us began our lives (We will both be 56 this year.)
1975 We committed our lives to the Lord on our wedding day, May 10.
1975 Following dental school, we moved to the mountains of NC [Now we know that this was God!]
1985 We made our first short term mission trip. [God had placed a desire in each of our hearts for this.]
1991 We sold our dental office and decided to give the Lord 2 ½ years of our life in Bible School.
1994 Our family made the move to Guatemala, Central America [after 14 short term trips!]

We have seen God touch thousands of lives through

dental and medical missions. Roger has had the opportunity to work on peoples' teeth in over 75 villages here in Guatemala, as well as many countries in Central America. Together, Roger, a general dentist and myself, Beth, a dental hygienist do check ups, cleanings, extractions and fillings for the children in a variety of mission organizations. As a result of working in one of these settings, we were introduced and challenged to consider work among squatters in a very poor squatters' settlement. We began a work to evangelize the people of La Primavera in the spring of 2000. This was followed with developing a feeding program for children that are sponsored through our non-profit organization, Hearts for Heaven, Inc. In October 2000, we began feeding the children that have been sponsored for the program three lunches a week. The children love it!

On Sunday afternoons, we also have a dynamic time with the children in this squatters' settlement. During this time we continue to touch the children individually with the love of the Lord through songs, drama, a lesson and craft time. God's love has truly made an impact on not only the children, but the families as well! Many of these children do not have opportunity to ever attend school; so we are praying about developing a school. Within our program are twelve and thirteen year olds that cannot read or write their own name! This is seen throughout Guatemala!

By 2005, we have three other feeding centers modeled after LaPrimavera with over 600 children enrolled in the programs.

Another facet of the Hearts for Heaven ministry is hosting teams from the USA that come down for 10-14 days to help out with construction, medical/dental and evangelism. Although this activity is exhausting at times, God touches all of our lives during these rich times of sharing with those that have so little!

During our eleven years here in Guatemala, we have been closely connected to the missionary school. Roger has served on the school board the last few years and also helped to head up two major fund raisers for the school's first gymnasium. Beth has taught elementary PE on a part-time basis four years and continues to help out with the band and small discipleship groups with the high school girls.

All four of our children from the oldest, John Paul, to the youngest, Sarah Kathryn, have each graduated from high school here in Guatemala and gone on to Lee University in Cleveland, TN. The three older children have completed studies at Lee and moved on to higher ground. John is presently serving with the Peace Corps for two years in Nicaragua. Rachel is working in the Knox County Health Department and Rebekah is enrolled in the Physician's Assistant Program at Emory University. Sarah Kathryn is presently a freshman at Lee. Like her older siblings, she would be quick to share with you that living in a third world nation has been a wonderful opportunity to learn another language and see firsthand how other people live.

Although there are certainly dangers that we as a family face regularly here in Guatemala; the opportunity to touch and impact lives that are less fortunate than ourselves far outweighs the hardships! By stretching ourselves, we have allowed God to use us in a greater fashion to challenge people to be all that God wants them to be. Although we lived a good life in the US (18 years of private dentistry and beginning a beautiful family) we do not imagine that we would have ever shared the love of God in the US to the degree that we have had opportunity here in Guatemala. We thank God for this opportunity to share His great love!

Roger has a neat story of a travel that he made down to El Salvador.49 Perhaps, I can get him to type it up for you. It was one of those occasions when one looks back and wonders if he has not been entertained by an angel of God!

Another spiritual example of God touching a life and turning it around (little by little) is little Carlos out at the settlement. Carlos is from a dysfunctional home. Each of the four siblings appears to have a different father. Mother is away at work 7am-7pm. As a result, Carlos has spent years on the street. When we first met him, it was obvious that he had been abused. At age 10, he was often seen sucking on his thumb (most probably a sign of deep insecurity.) As we began to build relationships with the huge variety of children at the settlement, Carlos would often burst into the scene and knock a child down. Singing or playing children's music would often cause him to behave very strangely. Whenever a group came to visit La Primavera, it wasn't long before everyone knew Carlos by name. He was a challenge to discipline. NO amount of love seemed to pacify him. He was a bright child that lacked greatly in opportunity.

As you might imagine, stealing occurs often in these poorer communities. A few years ago, Carlos' older sister, Evilyn carried a team member's bag to her house (instead of to our van.) When we discovered the mistake, Evilyn was approached, while the team sat in the van and prayed that God would work this situation out. We left with the contents of the bag, minus $100 that had been sent down by a church to bless someone. What appeared to be a damper to our wonderful time with the children was soon turned around. Upon arriving home, the team member discovered that the $100 had been tucked away in a suitcase. How does one handle unfair accusations?.... The next day, three of us took time out of our very busy day to return to Evilyn and Carlos' home so that WE COULD APOLOGIZE. This was done with a true spirit of humility and brokenness on our parts. The end result was that both Evilyn and Carlos kneeled in their door way and asked Jesus into their hearts.

Today Carlos is a different person. Oh, he still is called down and asked to sit still weekly in our children's' church and he has a huge propensity to beat on the other children. However, we believe that through the prayers of the believers that support this ministry and God's presence in this home, Carlos is a new creature. He memorizes the Bible verses and quickly responds to loving correction. Our prayer has now become, "Lord, let Carlos become a light to this desperate community—a life that was radically changed by the power of God's love!"

Carlos is one of the children that reflects a greater shift in growth and yet, as we look upon the children week after week, we can indeed see the results of the effectual, fervent prayers of the believers! As we work with the poorest of the poor here in this very poor nation, we love to share with them about a God that loves them every bit as much as He does the two missionaries, Beth and Roger, who came to share the love of God with them. God has no favorites. We are all equal in His eyes. And God has a plan, a wonderful plan for each of their lives!

"For I know the plan that I have for you, declares the Lord, plans to prosper you and not to harm you; plans to give you hope and a future." Jeremiah 29:11

Before I began to write (at much greater length that I originally planned), I thought it ideal for you to visit us; put on your recorder and just ask us questions. I imagine that you could fill in a lot of gaps!

Anyway, this is a start on sharing with you a little about ourselves. We do have a small brochure that we made and shared when we first came to the mission field nine years ago. The pictures are old; but the facts are the same. We can mail or scan this for you.

We trust that you are doing well and continue encouraged in God's great faithfulness.

In His Love,
Beth & Roger

The Scriptural View

As previously noted, over the decades, there have been several "It's not..." sayings that have embodied contemporary philosophies. In the 1970's, we had "It's not *what* you know, it's *who* you know." In school, there was "It's not *what* you know, it's *when* you know it." In the 1990's, I heard a business speaker say "It's not *what you know*, it's *who you trust*."

That last saying has, of course, always been true, and never more true than in our relationship with God. Roger and his family took a simple desire ("to help people") and entrusted it to God, as evidenced by Beth's reference to Jeremiah 29:11.50 Their desires did not involve material prosperity, as would be evident by their choice to work in a poor Appalachian community. However, along the way, God did reward them with a comfortable life. There are many applicable verses with respect to trusting in the Lord, but Psalms 37:3-6 seem to fit best:

"Trust in the Lord and do good;
Dwell in the land and enjoy safe pasture.
Delight yourself in the Lord
And he will give you the desires of your heart.

Commit your way to the Lord;
Trust in him and he will do this:
He will make your righteousness shine like the dawn,
The justice of your cause like the noonday sun."

Of course, the Briggs's also prepared for their task through their own educations, putting aside the temptations of the typical 1970's young lifestyles to become skilled in both their medical and ministerial abilities. In so doing, they evoked the teachings of 2 Timothy 2:21 "If a man cleanses himself of (ignoble purposes), he will be an instrument for noble purposes, made holy, useful to the Master and prepared to do any good work." Their preparation incorporated their children, in the true spirit of Joshua 24:15 (b) "...as for me and my household, we will serve the Lord."

TAXI ROBERT

El Salvador, as a country, has come a long way since the frightening civil war days portrayed in Oliver Stone's 1986 movie "Salvador." Dollarization51 of the economy, the advent of democratic elections, the passage of the Caribbean Basin Incentive,52 the building of arguably the nicest airport in the region outside of Panama, and many other developments have made the country one of the most desirable places to do business in Central America.

Concurrently, the imbalance of wealth typical in emerging nations, abetted by an earthquake in the year 2000, have made poverty, disease and lack of shelter an ongoing reality. Business travelers often stand in airport lines side by side with those on mission efforts; the suited and tied executive alongside the Wisconsin farmer clad in rigid denim overalls.

In May of 2001, I paid a visit to some local customers who supplied garments to American retailers under the advantages of the trade pact mentioned above. My companion was our company's international salesman who, being extremely well versed in the dangers of Central American travel, had hired a local man to drive us to our appointments. The driver's name was Roberto Martinez. Roberto, as required by his profession (part chauffeur, part bodyguard) was a large well-muscled man. His business card bore words "Taxi Robert—Speak English."

As midday approached, we decided to eat lunch in a place

of Robert's choosing. The little open-air grill was roofed with an old parachute, with walls about waist high, there being no real reason to protect from any weather elements other than rain. A very sad and inoperable "off white" ceiling fan with weeping willow angled blades hung high overhead, at the zenith of the 'chute. The floor was ash colored gravel. I would not have eaten anywhere else in the world.

Robert consulted with the cooks as to what would be their best fare for the day. He was obviously a frequent customer, and all involved were anxious to please his "important" American guests. We had a very pleasant meal, although I confess I never knew exactly what meat we were served, nor did it make me ill in the slightest.

I took a seat across from Robert. As we were served, I bent my head in a silent blessing. When I opened my eyes, I was surprised to see Robert gesturing at me with a very large ketchup bottle. My quick reaction was that he was being menacing, but a look into his soft eyes revealed that he was only trying to get my attention. "Where you go to church?" he asked sincerely. I explained that I was a believer in a large Baptist church in a major American metropolitan area. Robert's response was to tell me the story of his own salvation, which redeemed him from a long period of alcoholism, infidelity, a divorce, and other sad events which had alienated him from the most cherished person in his life, his 21-year-old daughter. I was delighted to hear that his conversion to Christianity had been the stepping-stone for reuniting him with the young lady. He shared many stories about the richness of their current life together. He gave me a small pamphlet that promoted the local church to which he belonged. If Robert had a "significant other," he made absolutely no mention of it.

In my job, I get told a lot of things that aren't true. Most of the time, I can tell if they are, or aren't. I would invest quite a bit of money, on the opportunity of a very small return, on the collateral of Mr. Martinez story.

When Robert delivered us to the airport, a business discussion broke out between Robert and our salesman as to the value of his services. It was decided that he would be paid less than originally contracted, as some of the appointments had been cancelled. Given the circumstances, I might have expected our valet to turn to me to cash in on the lunchtime narrative. Much to my peace, Robert did not disappoint me; he simply turned back toward his old car with its cliché coat hanger antennae. I had to chase him down to give him a pitifully insufficient tip. My reward was a giant hug.

Postscript

Standing on line at the San Salvador airport produced a continuation of the business/witness commingling experience, as there beside us were three distinct looking gentlemen. Wearing straw hats, very rigid denim overalls seldom seen today, and bearing long gray beards. A farm owner from Minnesota, engaged in the production of maple syrup, his son, and his foreman. I learned they were there on mission to help with the cleanup and rebuilding following the aforementioned earthquake. We enjoyed a brief sharing of our various experiences in Latin America.

Such airport dialog is very common in Central and South America. On one memorable occasion, I was passing through the Houston airport on return from a business trip to Honduras. As I waited to have my passport stamped, at the end of the long line, I noticed the immigration officer heading back toward me. He politely asked me to close the line to further passengers, whereupon he briskly returned to his position. Everyone in line looked at me curiously, then kidded me, wondering if I could enforce the order. I got some pretty strange looks as, one after one; I turned away new people trying to enter the line. One man wanted to stand in the line anyway, but I convinced him not to. As I neared the immigration station, everyone slapped me on the back and congratulated me on what a good job I had done, and how politely I had handled it. I made reference to having tried it the way Jesus would have, whereupon the lady in front of me told the story of her ministry efforts in Honduras.

Cora Adams, I don't know where you are today, but I pray the hospital that your church acquired in La Misquito is up and running and doing the Lord's work in both the body and the hearts of the local Hondurans. I hope that someday you will read this and let me hear from you. God Bless.

KEVIN

During the first several weeks of the divorce process, in the evenings, I would often lie on the couch, face to the upholstery, back to the world. On one such night in December 1998, there was a knock at the garage door. My family was still living at home at the time, and they admitted the visitor, our next-door neighbor Kevin Beckett. He moved gingerly through them, toward me, very much as if carefully passing between three statues.

Kevin was, at the time, about 40 years old (and therefore is my junior by about a decade) and a lifelong bachelor. You would have had to work pretty hard to be unaware that Kevin was a Believer. He was known throughout the neighborhood as a dedicated member of the singles class at Warren Baptist.

As I recall, that evening he did not so much *ask* me, but rather *told* me to meet him in his driveway that Sunday morning. I *was* going to go with him to church.

To me, Kevin always embodied what it meant to be bold for the Lord (the attribute I emphasized to my class of 10th grade Sunday School boys). To so many of us, witnessing comes uneasily. In that vein, one particular mental image will be with me always. A group of us from church were standing across the street from a motorcycle rally, its membership replete with tattoos, leather, chrome, and big loud bikes. I heard Kevin say "Let's go see if those folks are saved" and the next thing I knew, he was in their midst. None of the rest of us had the courage to join him. His visit prompted several of the attendees to produce two-inch by three-inch cards that identified a Christian group to which they already belonged, and fellowship sprung forth at once. ("Telemarketers" also seemed to bring out Kevin's boldness, the verse about Jesus and the moneychangers seemed to possess him when those phone calls arrived.)

As preparation for this text, I recently asked Kevin to share his most cherished scripture verses, and experiences and views on witnessing. He replied with this:

"I know a lot of scripture verses, more by context than by heart, but one sticks in mind and seems to come up more often than others, especially by others, whether a sermon or in passing or in a talk show on the radio.

I was talking with an acquaintance in New York State. I was living in Connecticut at the time. We had gotten on the topic of church and religion. I was a new Christian, so was eager to discuss. She responded that there were 3 very sensitive topics that cause consternation when discussed. They are politics, abortion and religion. I don't recall how I came across the verse, maybe using a concordance or a search in my study bible, or heard it in a sermon, but it is an excellent reminder of how to proceed when given an opportunity to share. The verse is 1 Peter 3:15 "But in your hearts set apart Christ as Lord. Always be prepared to give an answer to everyone who asks you to give the reason for the hope that you have. But do this with gentleness and respect". As you know Norm, I can get overzealous when I have the chance to share, so I need to be tempered by this verse. I think we all have the capacity to discuss any topic with this verse in mind. Where it gets sensitive is when we try to convince others instead of just presenting the facts or when we try to show them the errors or flaws of their opinions or beliefs. We need to remember to be available when God presents these opportunities to us and keep in mind that God does the work through us, not us doing the work for God.

Another interesting point Norm, is that I went to Our Daily Bread (today's devotional) to do a search for the actual verse I wanted to tell you about and lo and behold today's devotional is:

October 28, 2002
"Always Be Ready"
Read: 1 Peter 3:13-17

Always be ready to give a defense to everyone who asks you a reason for the hope that is in you.—1 Peter 3:15

I was concerned about my neighbor's spiritual health because he had been in such poor physical health. So one day I asked him, "Are you ready to meet God? If something were to happen to you, are you ready?" To my delight, he answered, "Yes, I took care of that." And he proceeded to tell me that he had trusted Jesus as Savior when he was a teenager. As we continued to talk, though, I found out he had some serious questions about the Bible and how everything fits together. He asked about God, Satan, sin, and the existence of evil in the world. I answered his questions the best I could, but that wasn't the way I thought the conversation would go.

Thankfully, my neighbor was a believer and was open to the things of God. Some people, though, can be antagonistic and may have the desire to mock or persecute us. Peter said that when such people ask us questions about our faith, we should "always be ready"-ready to explain our faith and hope in Christ (1 Peter 3:15). But to do so effectively, we must answer our questioners with gentleness and courtesy, not with harshness or disrespect.

"We may not always be persecuted for or questioned about our faith, but we should always be ready!"—Dave Branon

When people ask about our faith,
What answer will we give?
We'll tell of Christ who bore our sins
And shows us how to live.—Fitzhugh

Those who have questions about Christ need someone who has the answers.

How about that Norm!"

Although, in some areas, Kevin and I had very different views on scripture and matters of the faith, we became very compatible accountability partners. After reading what he says above, this will not come as a surprise. Although more fundamental than I, he always seemed willing to listen to my opinions, and our time together sharing the Word was very precious to me. And, though quite a bit older, I gained far more than he from the partnership, I am sure.

We had one very big thing in common: both of us were geographically a long way from anyone who might remotely be called "family" in the sense of blood relatives. For the most part, "family" to he and I meant the fellowship of our local brothers and sisters in Christ. Kevin was a Canadian, now living in the Deep South. While very respectful of "us Southerners," I believe he did think us a bit soft. His accent, affinity for hockey, use of the word "eh," reference to "ice" as "thick water," and habit of taking off his shoes at the door were not things local folks were used to seeing and hearing every day. Of course, in so many ways, that just made his work for God more effective.

One of Kevin's favorite possessions was a coffee mug that bore the following translation of his surname, and brief history of a previous possessor of it:

KEVIN
"Handsome by Birth"

"St. Kevin was the sixth century Abbot of Glendalough, Ireland, 'the valley of the two lakes.' The ruins of this abbey are still a favourite day trip from Dublin. The saint is reported to have lived a hermit and to have thrown a young lady who visited him into the lake. His supports, however, deny this saying that he merely beat her with nettles."

This seemingly out of character sentiment provided a clear window to the sense of humor of its owner.

If any one person was entrusted to save my life during some very dark days, I see that God entrusted Kevin to do that. And, as He always does, God knew who He was trusting.

The Scriptural View: Being Bold for the Lord

I would add these verses to those already quoted above:

Psalms 138:3 "In the day when I cried out, You answered me, And made me *bold* with strength in my soul."

Proverbs 18:1 "The wicked flee when no man pursueth: but the righteous are *bold* as a lion."

Acts 13:46 "Then Paul and Barnabas waxed *bold*, and

said, It was necessary that the word of God should first have been spoken to you: but seeing ye put it from you, and judge yourselves unworthy of everlasting life, lo, we turn to the Gentiles."

Romans 10:20 "But Esaias is very *bold*, and saith, I was found of them that sought me not; I was made manifest unto them that asked not after me."

2 Corinthians 10:1 "Now I Paul myself beseech you by the meekness and gentleness of Christ, who in presence (am) base among you, but being absent am *bold* toward you"

2 Corinthians 10:2 "But I beseech (you), that I may not be *bold* when I am present with that confidence, wherewith I think to be *bold* against some, which think of us as if we walked according to the flesh."

Philippians 1:14 "And many of the brethren in the Lord, waxing confident by my bonds, are much more *bold* to speak the word without fear."

1 Thessalonians 2:2 "But even after that we had suffered before, and were shamefully entreated, as ye know, at Philippi, we were *bold* in our God to speak unto you the gospel of God with much contention."

"DISNEY DADS"

I'm not sure if I should call it a temptation, a challenge, a tendency, or what. I do believe it is an almost universal truth. Divorced fathers, having usually lost primary custody of their children, will be faced with the "Disney Dad syndrome." We will want to "buy" our kid's love with laptop computers, fancy vacations, the latest in video and audio equipment, and so on.

This mentality is a poison to the recovery and growth of everyone involved. The children suffer most, especially the boys who opt for their father's custody when they reach an age where they have this choice.53 We have all seen many mothers of good disciplinary habits put aside in favor of fathers who could simply buy more stuff.

To be sure, during marriage, I treated the family to some nice, expensive vacations, often more than we could really afford. My excuse to myself was that I wanted the girls to be "worldly" and, indeed, that was part of it. But some of it was also selfish and very much "live for today." So I speak with no sense of smugness here.

I was very pleased, though, to experience a very different sort of post-divorce "resurrection" in my life with my daughters. In our years together as a family, we had constantly been involved in mission projects of one type or the other. With friends, we took a paintbrush to many things (among them the sanctuary of a small Tennessee Methodist church, the storage building of the Nashville homeless shelter), fed and fellowshipped with the homeless, and so on.

Following the fracture of divorce, it was quite some time before enough healing set in for me to be together with both daughters at the same time. When God led that to occur, His choice for the sacred place was this: an urban church, old and tattered *on the outside,* where various local congregations participated in a medical mission for needy families and a carnival for underprivileged children. The latter activity was one of those deals where you make it impossible for the kids *not* to win something. I watched over a monstrous laundry basket at which children threw basketballs from three feet away. To my left, Kelly ran the plastic duck pond where simply pulling out a rubber duck entitled the prize written at the bottom. To my right, Whitney and a young man of similar age supervised a ring toss game, where the object was to get a large hula-hoop over a pretty small inflatable porpoise. It was one of the happiest moments of my life.

(Note: The mission was an activity of Miracle Making Ministries in Augusta, GA., which is covered elsewhere here in its own chapter.)

THE "WISDOM" OF THE COMIC STRIPS

Wisdom can come to us through some unorthodox sources. Among those, we should not overlook the cartoon sections of our local papers.

Pride

The Pulitzer Prize winning comic "Doonesbury," by Garry Trudeau, is most well known for its controversial political messages. However, one particular strip was also the source of a brilliant parable on the term "pride goeth before the fall" (literally).

In the cartoon panel, two leaves, invested with the human qualities of thought speech, hang upside down from a tree branch. The leaf on the left, observing that autumn is approaching, launches into a discourse on the fatal chemical changes that he (and his companion) will soon undergo. It goes something like this: "We're deciduous," he explains to his partner. "As our host prepares for the winter, a wall of cork will form between the twig and our leaf stem. It will block the flow of minerals and water. Cut off from these nutrients, we'll stop forming chlorophyll." As the leaf goes on to describe the remaining consequences, the leaf on the right gradually realizes that these changes equate to his impending death. In shock, he replies, "That can't happen to me, *I jog!*"

This tale of woe says so much about the evils of too much belief in ourselves. On so many occasions, I've watched someone else's struggles, on the job, in a relationship, with their children, and have been overcome with the smugness of my own "success." Invariably, God humbled me by submitting me to the exact same struggle.

The Creation Story

Without questioning the literal truths of Genesis, a realistic view of the human race might cause us to consider Gary Larson's *Far Side* version of the creation story. On the ground, there is a large broken glass jar marked "Humans." The former occupants of the jar, clad in loincloths, are running loose across the verdant landscape, arms raised upward (but not in reverence to their Creator). A "thought balloon," with its arrow pointed upward to its Originator, bears the words "Uh-Oh!"

ROBERT L. WILLIAMS AND MIRACLE MAKING MINISTRIES

Many people find it hard, if not impossible, to embrace the citizens of underprivileged society, with their raw bristled faces, their yellowing or missing teeth, and their enormous needs. For those relative few who God bestowed with the gift of ministry to these, he bestowed it in abundance. It is as though he took all the love missing from the many and poured it all into the few.

Robert Williams is one of these treasured few. His lifelong commitment to the inner-city homeless and "near homeless" is inspired by James 1:27: "Pure religion and undefiled before God the Father is this: to visit the fatherless and widows in their affliction.............." His efforts in this direction have manifested themselves in many endeavors, the most significant of which is Miracle Making Ministries in Augusta, GA. Robert's love for those he serves magnificently issues forth at all times I have encountered him; in his words, in his actions, and simply in his being. There is nothing about his approach that is dramatic, it is simply a soft spoken manifestation of his love for a body of otherwise disenfranchised souls. His inspiration is derived from

An Augusta native, saved at the age of 6, his early "congregation" consisted of his little brother and sister; his "microphone" was a broom. After attending an "all black" elementary school for seven years, he was presented with the first of many important life decisions: he had a choice of middle schools, one "all black," one almost entirely "all white." A choice of the latter, he knew, would present him with the usual challenges of all pioneers, especially in these early days of integration where, in the Deep South, the word was much more of an ideal than a reality. Nonetheless, he chose the latter. He wanted the best public education he could get and, as he watched the world around him, he was able to see that an education at an "all black" institution would not prepare him for a society that was not all black and quickly changing. He followed the same inclination years later when given a choice of high schools.54

Upon graduation from high school in 1974, he spent five years pursuing his secondary "love," one that brought necessary immediate financial support, working with his father as an automobile mechanic.55 He then found more steady work in a local power plant. In 1979, he married Theresa Pinkston, at the unusual hour of 5:00 AM, so he would have time to return to his regular job and to make overtime pay. On the day that he met Theresa, the Lord had led him to begin the practice of tithing. Shortly thereafter, unhappy with "the way he was" (in his words), he heeded the call to the ministry that the broom had signified, and preached his first sermon in 1980.

Robert and Theresa then headed off to Jacksonville, Florida, where he had enrolled in Luther Rice Bible College. He recalls opening the small half-filled rented trailer at a state border agricultural checkpoint, and being reminded of the meagerness of his physical possessions. Upon graduation, he interviewed at a church in Savannah, Georgia, where his ideas about a "non-traditional ministry" (to go out and find the lost rather than waiting for them to find the church) were not accepted. After a short argument with God, which God won, Robert decided to pursue his Master of Divinity at Mid-America Baptist Theological Seminary in Memphis, Tennessee. Here again, the trip itself was memorable. Having to tow his 1964 Chevrolet behind his trailer, stops for gasoline became a constant necessity, and the Chevy lost its drive shaft as the family crossed the Mississippi-Tennessee line. Regrettably, Robert was correct that this was not a good omen for his time in Tennessee.

During seminary, he attempted to serve as part time minister of education for a local church, but issues of race (his choice, again, to attend a predominately white institution) and Biblical views (the church was liberal in its teachings) prevented this. Robert tried to support the family, now including daughter Rania, as a night auditor at a motel, and as a "mobile mechanic." The weather was colder than he had ever experienced, and he found his energy level dropping away almost daily. He soon learned that he was not just exhausted, he was very ill. Ultimately he checked into a hospital, where (although a young non-smoker) he was diagnosed with lung cancer. For seven consecutive days, the doctor[56] came into his room, examined him, and repeated his belief that Robert was dying. Finally, on the eighth day, the doctor returned with a diagnosis that Robert had "Mississippi Delta Blackbird Fever" (medical term: hystoplasmosis) which was caused by bacteria from bird feces. Treatment, at a cost of $615 per month, more than the family's housing payments, ultimately returned him to full health. During his recovery, he watched on TV (in horror) one of those events that people always seem to remember where they were when it happened: the explosion of the shuttle Challenger.

Graduation from seminary came in 1988, and the family

was soon blessed with a second child, a son named Jared. The Lord led them back to Augusta where, for a time, Robert's "see no color in the children of God" beliefs again met resistance from those whose vision was more clouded. Serving as the youngest senior pastor in the history of a 200-year-old traditional black church, he again found himself unable to carry out a ministry of change. But, as so often happens in such times of trial, the seeds planted earlier bore fruits of fulfillment. Out of the ashes of perceived failure, Robert and Theresa founded "Miracles in the Making," an outreach endeavor so named because of their belief that every person saved is a flowering miracle. From a mobile chapel, they spread the gospel of this mission until another key development: merger with a white minister's similar program in 1996. The ultimate result was a cross-cultural congregation of 600 that became "Miracle Making Ministries." In Robert's words, the mission statement of MMM is to "change the local community...one heart at a time." And, in terms that speak more to the functionality of the effort, "To be the vehicle by which evangelical believers move from their seats to the streets for the purpose of evangelism." And believers of all cultures at that.

My own particular miracle came when God's choice for the sacred place of reunion with my children was an MMM activity. The year was 1999, and I had not been together with both girls at the same time for several months. To picture the scene, imagine an urban church (named the Trinity Outreach Mission), its *physical* properties a bit run down, but not its *spiritual* properties. The yard is peopled with various local congregations; some garbed in "scrubs" participating in a medical mission for needy families, others working a carnival for underprivileged children. The latter activity was one of those deals where you make it impossible for the kids *not* to win something. I watched over a monstrous laundry basket at which children threw basketballs from three feet away. To my left, Kelly ran the plastic duck pond where simply pulling out a rubber duck entitled the prize written at the bottom. To my right, Whitney and a young man about her age supervised a ring toss game, where the object was to get a large hula-hoop over a pretty small inflatable porpoise. It was one of the happiest moment of my life.57

Today, MMM consists of four individual projects engaged in living execution of Robert's dream. The "Paul/Timothy Project" fosters the planting of churches and the training of pastors and lay people. Activities include a "Barbershop Bible Study," where men gather once a week for free haircuts and Biblical instruction. The "Miriam Ruth Project" protects "at risk" people, mostly women, from various endangers, often including death threats. The "Nehemiah Project" seeks reclamation of ghetto communities through Biblical principles. This ministry owns some 40 properties, which are being converted to safe affordable housing. Lastly, the "Apostle's Project" builds bridges between blacks and whites, Gentiles and Jews, through racial rehabilitation. Activities include community-wide worship events, youth conferences, and Race Relation Day messages.58

In one year alone, achievements by MMM in the Central Savannah River Area (as the metropolitan area surrounding Augusta is known) included the following:

- Guided 16,534 hours of volunteer efforts
- Served 3,189 meals
- Tutored 1,890 children
- Assisted 63 families in various emergency situations

- Fitted 263 people with eyeglasses
- Attended 327 medical needs
-

The story of Robert Williams' life is clearly a testimonial to the glow of God's love, shining through him, for his particular congregation. But it is also a testimonial to the miracle of perseverance. Usually, when we think of prejudice, we think of one person being set against another purely on a difference in skin color, or some other ethnic issue. Robert's trials came largely from prejudice of a different type: failure to accept another person's absence of prejudice.59 The road was long. As is true with many of the biographies presented here, a dedication to dream, principles and faith may require a lot of exposure to "wrong" before "rightness in God" can be experienced. But Robert has enjoyed, and been able to share with others, the fruits of his perseverance.

Postscript

My own introduction to working with homeless came at the age of 34, when I worked in the ministries of a church network in Greensboro, N. C. Every city seems to have its own way of dealing with the opportunity. This particular group of churches supported a "single site" location, and old abandoned grocery store, where the local impoverished were housed. Congregations took turns sending overnight teams to support the efforts of the one full time staff member, a lady named Joan. Joan was quite experienced and wise in the ways of her flock. Like Robert, she was loving and caring, but knew when to caress, when to coax, when to admonish, and when to just plain old intimidate.

My fledgling efforts at this are unforgettable to me. On

my first night of service, she dispatched me to clear the men from the bathroom (the only place where smoking was allowed) into their beds, the appointed hour for such having arrived. I charged into the thick tobacco perfumed haze and boldly commanded the necessary action. Some of the men turned toward me, barely moving. The few who responded verbally simply told me to shut up. I returned to Joan's office, defeated. She looked at me gently and encouraged "You're a man, you can get them out of there." Back I went, this time less aggressively, my approach being that they could help get Joan off *my* back if they would comply. Same response, perhaps even more unsympathetically. Again I retreated to Joan. Sighing, she rose and walked past me, opened the men's room door, and blasted out four words: "Get to bed, NOW!" Everyone was prone in his well-worn mattress in a matter of minutes.

STONES

From the first touch of God's finger bestowing life, we embark on fulfilling his mission for us on earth. An important realization, one we must come to grips with at an early stage, is that the road will be long and hard. As believers, we are tempted to think that God will reward us by making our path easier. Compared to non-believers, we might think that we will "automatically" have fewer incidences of serious disease, our children will give us fewer headaches, our marriages will be less challenging, and our careers will be more successful, and so on.

There are, of course, few if any statistics to support this. For example, the divorce rate today is not much different for professing Christians than it is for others. At least in part, this is undoubtedly due to our failure to practice our beliefs. However, it is also true that believers have no more assurance of an "easy" life than do any other sinners. The prayer concern lists that circulate among my Sunday School group bear this out.

In fact, living to God's standards almost assures us of *heavier* burdens than those who do not hew to the higher call. We accept responsibilities that others shun, question the ethics of situations that others merely accept, and often bear rebuke for doing so. Even the strongest believers I know occasionally ask themselves why they practice their beliefs when others seem so "happy" doing otherwise.

Lawrence Kimbrough expressed our burden with great eloquence in his book *Words to Die For*. "If you were expecting Christian life to be a pleasure trip, someone was guilty of false advertising. Being faithful to God and His Word will always come at a price. Sure, some will applaud your godly virtue, but you'll have plenty of others to malign your character and question our motives. The reward of the righteous rarely comes from the crowd but always from Christ. And that's reward enough." (See *Anyway,* Isaiah 66:5-6, John15:18-25, 2 Timothy 3:10-17).

I suppose I inherited it from my dad, but I often sought out challenges in life that tested my ability to carry burdens. Early in life, it was as simple as being the 110-pound kid carrying the 40 pound bags of oil dry (*South Carolina*). Later, it came in the form of professional challenges that would push my career growth. One such challenge, I believe the toughest one, is chronicled here.

I was offered a job that very few people were sure I could handle. The previous occupant of the position, a well-liked and respected man, had suffered an unfortunate fate. Many in the industry simply felt that *no one* should try to fill the job. As I considered the opportunity, I received all kinds of warnings from others: I as not going to like the job, I was going to be overruled too many times by upper management, my office would be too small, there were too may credit problem accounts, and so on.

I weighed these things, prayed about them, talked to family about them, and ultimately reached a decision to accept the offer.

My new employers were concerned that my old company would try to retain me with a higher salary, and that a "bidding war" would ensue. They asked how I could prevent that. I explained that this was very simple. Having accepted the position, I would be a man of my word and, to eliminate temptation, I would not disclose the amount of the offer to the old company. This strategy was successful.

I quickly learned that the problems pointed out by my friends were easily the least of my worries. To put it simply, I faced enormous pressure on many fronts, none of which involved my bosses, who were fair and free with me in my autonomy. Some of the pressure came from my staff members, who were either disappointed at not being offered the position, or who had internal political connections which they felt exempted them from my management practices. Some of it came from the sales department, which wanted to maintain the liberal credit policies of the past. On one memorable occasion, an obvious snub, one of the salesmen invited my staff to lunch, without me. The issue, of course, was not hurt feelings or empty stomach on my part, but the power play inherent in the action.60

I would like to say that I was brave every day, stood tall and acted with complete courage. I wanted to be the "Carl Brown" of another chapter; the strong white-starched collar figure. As much as I yearned for that, it was absolutely not the case. On many occasions, I had to duck the bullets and save the fight for another day. Many nights, I went home, upset with myself that I had not been stronger, but resolved to do better when the chance arose again. I prayed, a lot. I comforted myself with the memory of a sign that sat on my friend John F. Keller Jr.'s desk years before: "Ain't Nothin' Gonna Come Up Today That Me and The Lord Can't Handle." I begged God that, win or lose, I commit myself to doing the *right* thing in His sight. If I could not get things done my way, as His counsel showed me "right things" to be, I would at least voice my commitment and hope the seed would flower.

Over time, time that seemed an eternity, things began to change. My first "victory" was with the outside business community. Answering one of my prayers, I was shown a way to heal a wound by establishing a scholarship in the name of my fallen predecessor. This would not be issued in the name of the company, nor would I receive any credit, but rather we arranged for it to be issued by a business association. The recipient would receive free tuition and travel expenses to an annual legislative conference. A meeting was held to announce the scholarship.61

Inside the company, slowly, the ephemeral nature of "politics" gave way to the eternal power of rightness. Staffing changes and retirements within the company broke political connections which had weighed against me, but the effort to do the right thing still stood firm, and was remembered.

Some of those who were disappointed left the department. The process of recruiting to fill these slots taught me important lessons involving the values of flexibility, honesty, listening and maturity. When I tried to satisfy the definitions of the open positions, I rarely found candidates who perfectly fit. This forced me to assess the skills of the incoming candidates, weigh them against the skills of existing staff, and redefine both open and occupied positions to assemble the best overall team. This is where listening came in. Naturally, existing employees didn't always want their jobs redefined, or perhaps felt threatened by the talents of potential new employees. As the recruiting process went along, I met regularly with the impacted staff members, brought them up to date on our progress, and solicited their suggestions. One associate had an absolutely marvelous idea, one that permitted her to use her abilities in a way that had escaped me entirely. The result was a promotion for her and a new position that was ideal for one of the existing applicants.

On the matter of maturity, my preference was for people who were 100% committed if only 80% capable, instead of the other way around. Anybody devoted to this logical idea has fabulous role model in Bo Schembechler, athletic director and former coach of the University of Michigan. Near the end of the 1989 college basketball season, just prior to the beginning of tournament play, his coach (Bill Frieder) suddenly accepted a job with another university but offered to stay with Michigan through the playoffs. Schembechler's response: "I want a Michigan man to do the job." Schembechler handed the reigns to untested assistant coach Steve Fisher and, as any good NCAA basketball fan knows, the Wolverines won the championship.

Near the end of this period, in a very timely way, a business magazine called and asked me to write an article on merging two credit departments with differing business philosophies. "Write about the technical aspects, the software, describe which credit policy is best" they said. I said "yes," I would address those things, but what I would talk about most was the commitment to Jesus' principles of managing, and of dealing with people. Now, you know, of course, that an attribution to Jesus was not permitted in this format, so I had to do the best I could without that. This left me with the dedication to tell the story again, with the proper credit to the author of "right." Which, of course, is the story here in your hands.

Over time, Jesus' love manifested itself in ways I never imagined. I gained the acceptance of the sales team. We made many profitable and enjoyable business trips together.

Another rewarding moment occurred when I was able to rehire one of my recruits who had unwisely left the company in search of "greener grass." His family life having gone to shambles over his new and very heavy work schedule, he rejoined us when an opportunity arose. A few weeks later, he unexpectedly came into my office and said, "I want to tell you how much taking me back has meant to my life." Really, I deserved little or any credit; I had simply listened to the other associates who subtly let me know of his troubles. Nonetheless, his words were warm to my soul. I also saw from this experience that the flexibility and training used in forming and reforming the staff had created a local talent pool, from other associates who had left for various reasons. There were other occasions when the grass turned out to not be quite so green, and the rehires turned out to be "win-win" situations for both company and associate.

The Scriptural View

The issue of "office size" had an interesting conclusion. For the first several years, I operated out of my inherited office, which happened to be the smallest of any of the staff offices (as predicted). I dedicated myself to the idea that I rightfully didn't deserve anything better than those who supported me, and responded in that fashion when asked about it. Now, that didn't come naturally, but I tried to weld myself to the most selfless motive I was humanly capable of mustering. As I say, that did *not* come naturally. Ultimately, a spacious office became available. Several other managers clamored for possession of this "jewel." Ultimately, my boss called and reminded me that better surroundings would be of value to my interactions with visiting customers. Allowing me no choice in the matter, he insisted I move.

Now, if we DON'T handle something like this as Jesus would have done it, if we allow the slightest trace of manipulation to show through, regardless of how long we wait for the "jewel," we will be "found out" by others. Even in something as simple as this, it is plain to see how following His example will enable us to push aside our human frailties, our sin nature, our pride. Anything less would make us poorer leaders, less respected by our associates not only subordinate but peer and supervisor as well.

Listening has several essential components. The first is approachability; others must feel comfortable that their counsel is welcome, respected, and capable of producing a result. In 1 Samuel 3:10, the prophet gave audience to the Lord with the words "Speak, for your servant is listening." The second is to truly listen and to reflectively ponder on the speaker's words, drawing out clarification of any dimly understood passages. Proverbs 18:13 and 15 admonish speaking before listening and define the "ears of the wise" as those which will seek out knowledge. James 1:19 calls upon us to "be quick to listen, slow to speak, and slow to become angry." The third component is to act upon any agreement struck with the speaker, as Jeremiah stood at the gate of God's house and proclaimed His message (Jeremiah 7:2).

Surely enormous sections of the Bible speak to the value of maturity (Ephesians 4:13 and Colossians 4:12 among them), but the verses which admonish grumbling are perhaps most appropriate to office environs. James 5: 9 exhorts "Don't grumble against each other, brothers, or you will be judged..." Moses' was challenged often by grumbling masses (Numbers 14:29 and Exodus 15:24) and, with God's help, dealt effectively with the problem. Jude's travails are chronicled in his book; verses 16-21 prescribe a remedy. Paul responds with similar good advice in I Corinthians 1:10. Proverbs 27:3 speaks to the value of avoiding the provocation of fools.

A favorite secular encouragement to those in challenging circumstances is this advice: "Five percent of what happens to you in life is dictated by an event, 95 percent by your reaction to it."—Lou Holtz, football coach and motivational speaker.

Mary Anne Radmacher's famous quote provides another appropriate inspiration: "Courage doesn't always roar. Sometimes courage is the quiet voice at the end of the day saying, "I will try again tomorrow."

A final word on the concept of doing things the right way, in the Christian sense. A recent article in the science magazine *Discovery,* entitled "Whose Life Would You Save,"[62] is subtitled "Scientists say morality may be hardwired into our brains by evolution." (Really now?) As an example, the article cites cases where monkeys display their sense of "moral intuition" by taking up for themselves when slighted or deprived of what they regard as their fair share. For example, getting mad if they receive a treat that is less desirable than another monkey receives. Okay, the research may display a monkey's sense of *self-need* (see Maslow), I concede, but *morality?*

JIM AND BOBBY

Jim Overstreet is a tall, slender, mild mannered man, endowed with a self-admittedly childlike approach to life. He is an entrepreneur in the business of selling printed forms. As I read Brian Banashak's *Little Book of Business Wisdom,* Jim's face formed immediately in my mind. For such naivete and honor, he finds himself blessed with a beautiful Christian wife, Beth, a wonderful family, a successful business, a well deserved position as a deacon in our church, and a host of friends.

Jim was the first person, in the early days of my divorce, to help me get on the right road. By coincidence, with no knowledge of my situation, he called to let me know that he had been assigned to be the deacon for my alphabetic part of the congregation, and he wanted to have lunch. The fact that he was willing to drive over to my office, in a small town 25 miles from his office, impressed me greatly. The fact that he was even more anxious to do so once he learned of my distress impressed me even more.

Much later in the healing process, I talked to Jim about the material I was trying to put together. As I explained how I had been inspired in my maturity as a Christian man by A. J. Hewett, Jim shared with me the story below:

"It was great to visit with you yesterday, and I certainly hope we'll have that opportunity more frequently in the future! I mentioned to you how much I've enjoyed your collection of stories, and I wanted to pass along one of my own. The following is a portion of a letter that I received from my dear friend Robert E. Spence. He lived across the street from my family, and was like a grandfather to me. He was a very playful man, who genuinely loved people. In fact, he was one of the most other—oriented people I've ever met. Bobby, as I called him, was somewhat rough around the edges, but he, because of his good nature, to my knowledge didn't have one enemy on earth. In December of 1998, he was near the end of a long battle with cancer. This was something that none of his loved ones was ready to accept, including me. I was visiting my mom and dad one day when Bobby called and invited me over for a visit. He presented me with a small green box with the following label on top. "To J.W.: My Favorite Overstreet Caution: Highly Gender Sensitive Material. Instructions Inside. Do Not Open In The Presence Of

Anyone Of The Opposite Sex." He delivered this to me, naturally, in the presence of his sweet wife, Juanita. Both of them wore a grin at this point. Although his was much bigger, as though he had just won a bet with her. I quickly opened the box wondering what might lie inside. I found a letter which opened with a few things that are meaningful to myself and Bobby only. The rest of the letter follows: "Jim, the only thing I ever told you about women is that they are strange creatures. The reason I didn't tell you more is that after 49 ¾ years of marriage, I don't know much else.

In an effort to broaden my scope, I got on the internet and found a list of the continuing education courses offered at a popular institution of higher knowledge down in L. A. (lower Alabama). A list of these courses is attached for your edification. Unfortunately, I know absolutely nothing about any one of these subjects except #7 "bathroom etiquette II: His Razor is His." I wrote the book on this one.

Here's what I did after 30 years of scraping my face. I got myself an iron box and put a lock on it and then put my razor in it and kept the key in my personal possession at all times. After a few years I cured her of getting my razor. As you witnessed last week-end, she is in complete denial and pretends to know nothing about what I call the "razor episode." The main thing is that she is cured. To some that might not seem like much of an accomplishment, but to me it is a real breakthrough.

Jim, I have entrusted my intermost (sic) secret to you and I trust that you will treat it as such.

Please use this box as long as needed. I estimate that within 25 years Beth will get the message and by that time your daughters will be either married or away at Auburn.

When you get through with the box, please give it to Mike or Wesley, whichever one gets married first.

Your friend and admirer, Bob Spence"

The attachment to the letter was an e-mail titled "Continuing Education Courses For Women," and it was quite funny! The real reason Bobby gave me the box and the letter was to prepare me for his death. Bobby loved the Lord, and I know he is with Him now. I really believe that God allowed him the time and strength to put closure on some things in this life, and I'm so thankful for that. I want to share with you, also my very personal response to his gift. Bobby had given to me my entire life, and I realized that I was powerless to give anything in return short of sharing with him my great admiration of him. The letter I wrote in response to his gift follows:

"Dear Bobby,

I've had the little green box, and the letter you wrote me now for about two months. They are, as you are, a real treasure to me. This is my poor attempt to communicate that to you. When I consider my childhood, I'm really amazed that God blessed me so much. In some of my most awkward and unlovable times, you gave me an incredible gift...your time. To this day, when I'm in your company, I feel like the little boy I was not too many years ago. I hope that's a great compliment to you. In addition to learning that great truth about the strangeness of women, I also learned a great deal more from you, and your example. I would have never understood the virtues of Little Debbie's for breakfast or peanut butter soup without you. I've learned how to build go-carts, sign out tools, enjoy iced tea among many other things. I've learned that when your lawn mower stops running, you should change the air filter. Most importantly though, I've learned that nothing is junk. In the hands of the right craftsman, anything can be made beautiful. The Lord created a masterpiece in you. The world would be a much better place if more people were like you. I have very few heros. My standard is quite high. I want you to know, though, that you're on that list. I love you, and I'm proud to call you my friend.

God Bless You, J.W.

Later on that month, Bobby checked himself into hospice care. He fought bravely for several weeks. We brought him home for one more visit to his house, and his wife and daughter and grandchildren and friends visited him regularly at the hospice. One day, I believe it was late April '98, Bobby breathed his last. He was one of the greatest men I've ever known.

Thanks for letting me share his story with you.

Jim"

The Scriptural View

The Bible is, of course, filled to the brim with accounts of men and women who were friends to one another. Their friendships took on many forms and often changed over time. Some worked hand-in-hand, side-by-side as peers. Proverbs 18:24, Romans 15:2, and Ecclesiastes 4:8-12 embrace this concept. Some friends, such as David and Jonathan, enhanced the level of companionship with remarkable loyalty. Some friends rescued their counterparts from some danger or malady, such as Boaz for Ruth in Ruth 2, and Pharaoh's daughter for Moses in Exodus 2:5. Large scale rescues included Esther's rescue of the Hebrews in her book, and of course the ultimate in Jesus salvation of his congregation from the consequences of sin. Some scriptures speak to the concept of friends holding one another accountable, as in Proverbs 27:17. Some friends served as counselors or mentors to others (a prevailing theme of this book and, in its unique way, a theme in the story of Jim and Bobby).

Examples of this latter concept include the man who interpreted the friend's dream in Judges 7:13-15, and Joash's service as an example to Amaziah in 2 Kings 14. For Jim and Bobby, perhaps the best parallel lies in the stories of Elijah and Elisha. In 1 Kings 19:19, Elijah the prophet makes himself known to the younger Elisha by throwing his cloak across Elisha's shoulders as the young man tills his fields. Elisha is immediately caught in the web of the prophet's spirit and follows after him. The relationship culminates when Elijah, just prior to being swept into heaven by a whirlwind, asks Elisha what he can do for him before he is taken away. Elisha responds, "Let me inherit a double portion of your spirit" (2 Kings 2:9 NIV). As Elijah is drawn upward into heaven, the cloak falls to earth, and Elisha picks it up for his future use. Bobby's green box became Jim's version of the cloak.

I also recently found a marvelous parallel in a song by the country music duo Brooks and Dunn. It is called "Believe." Listen to it and you will "see" Bobby in the form of Old Man Wrigley.

THE SEAMSTRESS

There may be no individual mentioned here whom I miss more than my old friend Fred. When we were in our 30's, we were virtually inseparable, despite distinct differences in some of our value sets. For example, Fred was the consummate physical specimen, chiseled by his exercise regimen; I much more defined by my widening midsection. He was the only person I ever knew who often spent his Friday nights throwing a *javelin* for fun. He was also a diligent planner; the storage building he designed and built for his backyard was a marvel of geometry and amateur carpentry. We were bound only by our strong friendship and commonality of free spirit. Today, we are separated by a physical distance far too enormous to bridge.

There was nothing that we would not do for each other in those times. Our biggest project together was to lay about 30 yards of concrete driveway alongside his house one blistering summer day. At the end, I lay on the ground and pawed with my trowel at the last bit of concrete, already too dry to mold. The finished product looked a little too much like a corduroy road but it held up cars just fine. Mopping a little sweat from his forehead, Fred announced he was "a little tired," yet I was so exhausted that only a powerful muscle relaxer could halfway limber me enough for sleep.

Handsome and intelligent, with slightly balding red hair,

Fred got along with everyone and welcomed lively discourse on any topic, from politics to engineering. He had been a master of debate on his high school team. A transplanted New Jersey native, he was lured South by an education at the University of North Carolina, and stayed South when he found career here.

Fred and I were both married without children, although my two soon came along and developed their own strong bonds with him as they grew. He was "Uncle Fred." Ultimately, his marriage collapsed under the weight of nothing to come home to. He and Pam remained childless, and she developed her own set of hobbies to counter the loneliness created by his outside interests. His only known "failure," if it may be called that, came in the form of divorce. We worked together for the same company for many years, but ultimately this changed as his ambition took him into the field of stock brokerage.

One morning, as I sat in my office, the phone rang and the voice on the other end was my then-wife Karen crying uncontrollably. "Fred died" she finally choked out. "How?" I asked in response to the impossible statement. "He took his own life." I argued that someone must have broken in and killed him, to which she stated the obvious "Who would have chosen to confront him, of all people, at his home?"

In the next 48 hours, the incredible truth beat down my denial. Fred, in character, had carefully planned his death, lying down in his bathtub so as to soil his home as little as possible as he pulled the trigger on the rifle I didn't know he owned. He had called the police and told them what they would find when they came.

At the memorial service, we his friends were universally speechless, pallid, ashen, and unbelieving. His former secretary Kathy grabbed me as I entered and cried—"Why, Norman, why?" I had absolutely no answer. I approached his boss who stood nearby. "He was so strong, so confident" I offered. He dropped his head. "On the outside" was all he could say. The priest addressed our disbelief: "Many of you have come here tonight seeking answers. I do not have them either. You probably do not know that Fred had been coming to me for help (though counseling). The Fred that did this thing to himself is simply not the Fred you knew and loved." He spoke of the sin of Fred's act.

Little by little my friend Bobby and I made trips to the house to bring out things for people who could not bear to go. The interior was immaculate, as it always was, a tribute to any home, of bachelor or family. There were two identical sets of open manila envelopes on the kitchen table. The contents, apparently never used, were cassette tapes on the treatment of depression.

One particular day, Fred's dad (who we had never met) came down from New Jersey by plane. Solemn, strong of build, he met us in the lobby of the hotel where he was housed. Having no land transportation, he asked Bobby and me to take him to the house so he could get some special things. He rode in the backseat, silent and sad, although I felt sure he knew that we burned to know; did *he* know "why"? I will never forget one item we picked up, from under the bed, a cardboard box full of awards and accolades from Fred's schooldays.

On the way back to the hotel, the father's voice in the backseat suddenly began to speak. I was never sure why, I think our pain simply overcame his reluctance. Fred's dad explained to us that Fred had suffered from depression since he was 14. He had attempted suicide on at least one other occasion, and had purchased the rifle several years before with just that intention. The explanation made us understand history, we now knew that our friend had concealed a horrible secret for a long time. But we still did not know "why."

I thought of all the times that Fred and I had shared lunch, how I had moaned and groaned during those meals about all the things that bothered me, which was a lot. I thought of how he listened, apparently without a care of his own. Then I realized that, somehow, his simple inability to unload his own cares had single-handedly created a monstrous tragedy within his mind. I later learned that he had left behind several hours of audiotapes. In the tapes, he verbalized his enormous sadness and frustration at being unable to personally stop world hunger, disease, poverty, and many other ills. And he apparently mentioned how he admired me, the inferior grumbler, for being able to do that one simple thing.

I still think of Fred a lot. I think of him when the crisp October nights remind me of fun things we did together. I think of him whenever I see that a friend can't turn loose of his pride to share his burden. And I pray for his soul because one thing that we never discussed was salvation.

During the days soon after his death, I took some clothes over to Bonnie Norton's house. Bonnie was a retired former co-worker who did a little sewing to make ends meet. Her granddaughter was usually there playing around the porch of the little clapboard house. Bonnie kept the child when the mother was unable to support the little girl.

Bonnie walked out to meet me as I wrestled the clothes off the hook over the car door. The little yard, sparsely grassed, and the tiny house framed her kind face. "Did you hear about Fred?" I asked. She nodded, then shook her head in soft bewilderment. "Thirty two years old and nothing to live for. I'm sixty-five and I have everything to live for." In that instant, I came to understand a lot.

The Scriptural View

I could chase "The Holy Grail of Enoughness" and say, if I had just reached out to Fred in his pain, I could have prevented this. If I had been more like some of the friends chronicled in *Jim and Bobby*, I could have helped him more. But, generally, I know this is not true, like so many people, he just did too good a job of hiding his inner strife.

Rather, I will quote Luke 12:22-28 (NIV). In its towering eloquence, these scriptures explain the things that Bonnie understood so clearly. Things that some of the rest of us simply did not:

"Then Jesus said to his disciples, 'Therefore I tell you, do not worry about your life, what you will eat; or about your body, what you will wear. Life is more than food, and the body is more than clothes. Consider the ravens: they do not sow nor reap, they have no storeroom or barn; yet God feeds them. And how much more valuable are you than birds. Who of you by worrying can add a single hour to his life? Since you cannot do this very little thing, why do you worry about the rest?

"Consider how the lilies grow. They do not labor or spin. Yet I tell you, not even Solomon in all his splendor was dressed like one of these. If that is how God clothes the grass of the field, which is here today, and tomorrow is thrown into the fire, how much more will he clothe you, O you of little faith.'"

"LET'S HELP OUT A LITTLE SISTER…"

So said the "subject" line of the e-mail from my friend Vinny. Such mail from Vinny came as no surprise; he was always known to try to help someone out or spread a word of encouragement. To picture Vinny's physical appearance, first just imagine, well, someone named Vinny. The act of "stereotyping" people is seldom if ever put to much good use. However, in this case, the name "Vinny" has been consistently applied to recognizable media characters so often that it can't help but serve some purpose, at least as far as a physical picture is concerned. Dark-complected, salt and pepper hair, very nice looking guy, single. Night owl. *Wild at Heart.* More "spiritual" than "religious," in his own individual way.

One of my lasting recollections of Vinny occurred in the middle of a business meeting shortly after the tragedies of September 11, 2001. As a knot of assembled managers bemoaned the new complications of air travel, he hung his head in aggravation and said "Hey Norm, just don't travel with any guys that look like me!" Meaning, of course, that he bore a physical resemblance to certain of the terrorists displayed on television. While the marks of his Mediterranean origins are written clearly on his face, I had never considered, until then, how those marks could be interpreted as Middle Eastern rather than Italian. But, suddenly, I saw his point (he later decided that his beard was the problem, so he disposed of it). Personally,

I also had the luxury of knowing his *heart,* a vantage point that prevented me from thinking of him as anything resembling a terrorist.

At this point, I have to stop and remind myself this isn't a chapter on Vinny. His is a story to which we'll return but, first, the story of the "little sister," a little sister in Christ.

Vinny's email went on to read:

"Please Help!

This is a real science project, so help this little girl out. We should be thankful that there are kids out there trying to incorporate Christ into their science projects—wow!

February 7, 2003
Hello my name is Katie Kite and I am 10 years old. I go to _____ Elementary School in _____, ___, and I attend _____ Baptist Church.63 I am doing a Science Project to see how many people that I can reach on the Inter Net and how many of those people believe in Christ. I am trying to see how many people I can reach in just three weeks, so please help me. If you receive this please do these two things:

1. Please send an email to the following address kssciencprojec@aol.com please include your city, state and country, and if you believe in Christ. You do not need to include your name
2. Please forward this email to everyone on your mailing list. (will be keeping track of the number of response, as well as locations. Therefore, send it to everybody you know. In my project I am trying to

demonstrate how many people believe in Christ and how fast and far information can travel on the Inter net in a period of time. If you receive this email after February 28 please ignore it because the project will be over. Thank you all very much for your help and God Bless you.

Katie Kite"

Wow, indeed. It seems that everyone who owns a computer gets at least three or four "chain letter" type requests every day, the majority of which are quickly trashed (and we Christians are as guilty as anyone about flooding the internet with these), but this request was irresistible. The power of the witness and testimony, from such a young lady, was overwhelming.

The curiosity to know more about the young lady and her project compelled me to call her school, where I verified the authenticity of the request and learned that this approach was *entirely* her idea. I also contacted little Ms. Kite's mother, asking that she and Katie share with me the results of her efforts, to which she readily agreed.

Soon I was spreading her gospel message to friends and acquaintances in as many countries as I knew: the American Ambassador to Honduras, a businessman in Mexico, a sales agent in Italy, and so on. All were likewise touched and agreed to promptly respond to her with their testimonies of their own faith.

The results of Katie's survey were sent to me in April,

2003, and appear on the following pages. To preserve the authenticity of her work, the spelling and grammar is left just as presented to Katie.

PURPOSE

-
1. How Many People on the Internet Believe in Christ?
2. How Far Can the Internet reach in only three weeks?

HYPOTHESIS

-
I think that I will get about 20 e-mails from people that believe in Christ.

MATERIALS

-
I need to use a computer and the Internet.

RESPONSES

-
YES WE BELIEVE
(Cover sheet for the following testimonials)

In answer to a young lady's questiong, I am responding. I was 12 years of age when I asked the Lord Jesus to forgive and save me from my sins. He did. He has been my Lord and Savior for 63 years. I am trusting daily in His love divine, He is a Friend of mine. Yes, I believe in the Lord Jesus Christ, as the Son of God, as He is God who took on a human body so that He paid for the penalty of sin as demanded by a holy God. The Bible says "There is no name under heaven whereby we can be saved, except the name of Jesus." Geneva

Dear Katie,
Hope your e-mail site is still up and running as I wanted to congradulate you on a wonderful topic, and say as a Mom of 4 kids, two of whom have already done a science project, I will be remember your topic when our twins get to 3rd grade, the grade when their school begins science projects. What a wonderful witness. Hope your data and presentation was rewarding and that the Lord was glorified!!

Keep living for Jesus. And keep being an encourager!!
Fellow Believers in Christ,
The Farb Family (all six of us)

Yes, I not only believe in Christ, But he is also my personal Savior.
R&C, Wilmington, North Carolina

I have trusted Jesus Christ as my personal Savior.
Nancy. I'm from Tampa, Fl (but i'm in college in Greenville).
Hope your project goes well! God bless. Stay grounded in the Word?
Heb. 12:1-2

wow isnt that cool how many people believe in

christ?!?!?!?!?!?!?! i think it is and i think its really cool that you got 3rd good job. well i got to go so i will talk to youlater. bye
Katie

I am a born again christian,Ilive in a small village in Mill Run, Pa. and attend Mill Run United Methodist Church. I help out with the youth and children programs and enjoy serving the Savior. I am a U.S. citizen. I am a mother of 3 and grandmother of 7 and have been married 40 years the 16th of this month . God Bless

I live in Campeche, Mexico because my husband was transferred here with a textile company, we both are from spartanburg,sc.... goodluck with your project...and yes we are christians.. my husband , myself and our two children..
god bless,
lisa

Katie,
I know your project is over but I just wanted to thank you for believing in Christ and not being afraid to tell the world. You are an inspiration and may he be with you always.
Natalie

Thank you Katie for keeping me so well informed about your project! ALSO—CONGRADULATIONS on earning the third place at the fair!!! I am so VERY PROUD of you, and I pray that my little six year old grand daughter learns to love the Lord and does just as well as you have done in your science project!
Although it was a project for a worldly system, God still sees it and is smiling at you and I am sure that He will be rewarding you!!!
See you in Heaven, my little friend!

Love,
Marylin
Milford, Iowa

Survey Results

-

Date (2003)/No/Yes

-

February 08, 1 NO, 2 YES
February 09, 0 NO, 10 YES
February 10, 0 NO, 17 YES
February 11, 2 NO, 6 YES
February 12, 0 NO, 7 YES
February 13, 0 NO, 6 YES
February 14, 0 NO, 30 YES

Week One Total, 3 NO, 78 YES

February 15, 0 NO, 16 YES
February 16, 6 NO, 20 YES
February 17, 0 NO, 81 YES
February 18, 7 NO, 233 YES
February 19, 3 NO, 890 YES
February 20, 1 NO, 1,986 YES
February 21, 3 NO, 2,028 YES

Week Two Total, 20 NO, 5,254 YES

February 22, 2 NO, 1,980 YES

February 23, 0 NO, 2,317 YES
February 24, 17 NO, 2,702 YES
February 25, 0 NO, 4,403 YES
February 26, 1 NO, 5,309 YES
February 27, 3 NO, 5,857 YES
February 28, 2 NO, 4,329 YES

Week Three Total, 25 NO, 26,917 YES

FINAL TOTAL, *48* NO, *32,249* YES

STATES AND COUNTRIES

My village is McBride, BC Canada
Parsons Kansas USA
Valparaiso, IN USA,
Huber Heights, Oh 45424 USA
Gladstone, Oregon USA
Suisun City, CA USA
Statham, GA (USA)
Warsaw, Virginia
Ephrata, PA 17522-9639 USA
Goldthwaite, TX
Nunspeet, Holland
Cullowhee, North Carolina
Irmo, South Carolina USA
Pembroke, Massachusetts, United States of America
Middleboro MA
St. Paul, Minnesota
Glenrock, Wyoming, United States
San Juan, Puerto Rico
Deptford, NJ in the USA
Phoenix AZ USA
Hueytown, AL 35023, USA
Vero Beach, FL 32963
Charleston WV
Puyallup, Washington
Chariton, Iowa

Ellsworth, Michigan United States of America
Santarem, Para, Brazil
Galena, Missouri, USA
Norman, OK, United States
Nolensville, Tennessee USA
Geneseo, IL USA
Cortland, NY, USA
O'Fallon, MO USA
Culver, OR United States
Kelowna, province of British Columbia
Caribou, Maine
Riverview, NB
Managua, Nicaragua in Central America
Louisville, Kentucky, USA
Columbus, MS, USA
City—New Britain, state—Connecticut, country—USA
Greetings from New Ipswich NH
Little rock, Arkansas
Burlington, VT, USA
Hello from Heidelberg, Germany...we believe!
It's Feb 28th at about 5 to 9pm in Ireland
Japan
TWIN FALLS, IDAHO, USA
Buckinghamshire in England
Greeley, CO USA
Logan, Utah
Rapid City, South Dakota
New Orleans, La., USA YES!
Hermosillo, Sonora, Mexico
I am in Brazil
I am in Cheltenham, in Southern England
I live in Hiawatha, Kansas

GOD SPOKE AND HE SOUNDED LIKE....

Manitowoc, WI USA
I live in Waterville, Maine 04901, United States
I live in Kenai, Alaska, USA
I live in Bobo-Dioulasso, Burkina Faso, West Africa
City: Amman, Country: Jordan, Yes, I believe in Christ.
Cape Town which is one of the big cities in South Africa
Pecs Hungary
Rapid City, South Dakoata, United States of America
Marmaris, Turkey
Norgerweg 32, 8433 LN Haulerwijk, the Netherlands
From North Dakota
Keota, Iowa, Keokuk Co
City: Hockessin, State: Delaware, Country: USA
Honolulu, Hawaii, USA
Sibu, Sarawak, Malaysia
I'm from Singapore
Palmerston North, New Zealand
Portales, New Mexico, USA
I live in Montana
I live in the capital city of Kenya i.e. Nairobi.
Bandung, West Java, Indonesia
Wales, GB.
Aminogatan 27, 431 53 Mölndal, Sweden
Chiang Rai, Thailand
City: Antwerp country: Belgium
Manchester, Lancashire, UK
Hamburg, Germany
Country: Kosovo / Former Republic of Yugoslavia
9 Norlands Crescent, Chislehurst, Kent, United Kingdom
Livorno, Italy
Marmaris, Turkey

Soldotna, Alaska, USA!
Pahrump, NV Nye county, USA
I live in Volda (city) More & Romsdal (state) Norway (country).
In Rhode Island
Your email made it to me in Biloxi, Mississippi
Chiang Mai, Thailand
This is Calvary Chapel Smolensk, Russia
Gillette WY
Cornwall, England
Ulica Walczyka 22, 02-849 Warszawa, Poland
Rosemarie Birrenkott, Jamestown, ND 58401
Carson City Nevada USA
City, Glenrothes, State, Fife, Country, Scotland
In Phnom Penh, Cambodia
In Costa Rica
In Hong Kong,
From Uruguay
Menwith Hill, England UK
In Itimpi, Kitwe, Zambia, Africa
We live in Honolulu, Hawaii USA
Living in Chillan, Chile, South America
Bradford, Maine USA
I live in Romania, Europe, city—Resita
Sao Paulo, Sao Paulo, BRASIL
Pascagoula, Mississippi USA
Country = BARBADOS, LOCATION = West Indies/ CARIBBEAN
Georgetown, Grand Cayman, British West Indies
Monster that's in Holland
City: Cairns State: Queensland. Country: Australia
Greene, Maine, USA

GOD SPOKE AND HE SOUNDED LIKE....

I live in Tokyo, Japan
Time Reichenberg, Bavaria, Germany
I'm in London
Kosice, Slovakia Eastern Europe
In Brazil
Florence, Italy
Live in Quito Ecuador

CONCLUSION

-

The first week I received a total of 81 e-mails and three of them did not believe in Christ. The farthest e-mail I received for the first week came from Australia.

The second week I received a total of 5,274 e-mails and 20 of them did not believe in Christ and the farthest one came from Russia.

The third week I received a total of 26,942 e-mail and 25 of them did not believe in Christ. The e-mails by this came had come from all over the World.

I received a total of 32,249 e-mail from people that believed in Christ and a total of 48 e-mail from people that do not believe in Christ.

The complete total for the three weeks was 32,297 for believes and non-believes. The e-mail reached all 50 States and almost every Country around the World.

My conclusion is that people believes in Christ all over the World and that e-mails can travel anywhere in the World.

-Katie Kite

Katie clearly shattered her initial goal of 20 responses! The concluding statistics probably speak, in part, to the likelihood of Christians to respond affirmatively, rather than non-Christians to respond negatively to such a sweet message. There was probably also a tendency for Christians to focus on achieving a nice geographic spread for Katie, by writing to fellow Christians in other countries rather than to non-believers.

In other words, while bringing salvation to the lost was not the stated focus of the project, or maybe even the purpose that anyone pursued, the potential of such was surely inherent in the power of Katie's message. Even if only by blessed *accident*, it would be impossible for the message of Jesus to have *not* been aloft on Katie's wings. Imagine what the handful of non-Christians thought as just a small breath of the wind billowed around them.

As I worked with Katie's mother, entirely by e-mail so as to avoid intruding on their daily lives, some obvious questions occurred to me. Those questions were: how was this young person blessed to undertake such a project, and from what source did her Christian dedication come?

Somehow, I had the idea that the answer would not be the traditional story of long happy marriage, raised in church from birth, and so on. I don't know why, there were no clues; perhaps it is just the reality of a hard world and people coming to Jesus by times of trial. As my minister Bret Legg says, some meet

Jesus in the garden and some meet Him in the wilderness. To my questions, Katie's mother wrote the following:

"I did receive your first e-mail. It has been real busy around here. I have put a lot of thought into what you have asked...to be truthful with you the only way that I can explains Katie's salvation is by the hands of God. I grow up in a home were God was not talked about. In fact I did not go to church while I was growing up. I did not start going to Church until the girls were about 4&3 (Katie was four). Then I only went to keep their dad from beating me. After a while he started beating me for going. Katie only knows that if we went to church her daddy was going to hit mommy when we came home. So I finally quit going. A couple of years late, in 2000 I meet my Husband Robbie and we started talking and 2001 we started dating. Robbie keep talking to me about Church and I finally started taking the children to Church every Sunday and Wednesday with him. This was in October of 2001 and by June of 2002 Katie was saved and had talked to one of her friends, who started going to Church with us and she became saved and was Baptized at the same time as Katie. Because of God's will he lead to me to my Husband who showed us the way to ever lasting salvation. Because of God's will Katie does not remember coming home from Church and seeing me getting beat because we went. Katie is happy and Loves to go to Church. She does not have a problem of bring Christ and God up in a conversation. If you need anything else please just let me know.

Thank You and God Bless You,
April"

I explained to April that I would not share her story without her permission. Nothing that I could paraphrase or add could make any stronger statement than her response:

"I feel that my past has made me stronger and has made my faith that much stronger in the Lord. If it will help bring one person closer to the Lord and Savior, then all of the story was worth it. You may use all of it or any of it that you think might help. Katie and her Sister Kristine have not seen or talked to their father in over three years. On April 23, 2004 @ 10:00am we are going to court for the final hearing of the Adoption. Robbie will not just be there Daddy, he will be there Father. Katie and her Sister will be taking Robbie's last name, they will no long be a Kite."

Her story also reminded me of how Mary Duncan's failed marriage nonetheless spawned strong Christian offspring.

There are many appropriate Bible verses that apply to Katie's witness. The most appropriate are the verses involving "The Great Commission"; "Go ye into all the world, and preach the gospel to every creature" (Mark 16:15 KJV). And Matthew 28:19 (KJV) Go ye therefore, and teach all nations, baptizing them in the name of the Father, and of the Son, and of the Holy Ghost. (The complete set of relevant verses is Matthew 16: 15-18 and 28:16-20)

Another verse that leaps quickly to mind is Isaiah 11:6:

"The wolf will live with the lamb, the leopard will lie down with the goat, the calf and the lion and the yearling together, *and a little child will lead them.*" (NIV)

This verse of prophecy speaks specifically to the second coming of Jesus (the "little child"), in the Messianic age, which will produce tranquility to all the earth. Its application to Katie is most appropriate in the sense of the Christ-like nature of her actions.

Other relevant verses include:

Proverbs 20:11—"Even a child is known by his actions, by whether his conduct is right and pure." Surely Katie's behavior spoke to the purity and rightness of her conduct.

Proverbs 22:6—"Train a child in the way he should go, and when he is old he will not turn from it." A testimonial to the strength of Katie's mother and the support of her new husband.

Matthew 18:1-6—"At that time the disciples came to Jesus and asked: 'Who is the greatest in the kingdom of heaven?' He called a little child and had him stand among them. And he said 'I tell you the truth, unless you change and become like little children, you will never enter the kingdom of heaven. Therefore, whoever humbles himself like this child is the greatest in the kingdom of heaven? And whoever welcomes a little child like this in my name welcomes me. But if anyone causes one of these little ones who believe in me to sin, it would be better for him to have a large millstone hung around his neck and drowned in the depths of the sea."

Postscript

Let's return for a minute to our friend Vinny. Vin isn't necessarily much of a "Sunday Christian." Now, what does that mean? It means that, maybe, he isn't at church as much on Sundays as most "typical Christians" (a term that may beg a little defining).

However, his witness speaks loudly to me during the workweek. When he speaks Jesus' name, as he often does during the business day, there is an unquestionable sincerity. There is no doubt about the attribution, his salvation, his faith, and his *friendship*. And his embodiment of those characteristics goes well beyond a mere spreading of faith based e-mail messages. Indeed, the word "friendship" embodies Vinny; in the way I value my closest friends like Vin, I realize they are the people I would want beside me if I were in a war. Since we are all in a daily spiritual war, there is a very good reason for that valuation system!

Which prompts us to ask ourselves a question, we many who open up and lock down the church house on Sundays and charge ourselves to remember to speak God's message during the rest of the workweek. That question involves the idea of "image," the pervading idea in my story of Vinny. Without trivializing the need to be at church on the Sabbath, are we doing as well as Vinny when it comes to witnessing the "other six days"? Or are we too caught up in their failure to fit the "Sunday Christian" image?

"I DIDN'T PRAY AGAIN LAST NIGHT, REB."

Earl Ryals, friend and mentor, was a pretty regular contact of mine, so I wasn't surprised to get a call from him one Monday morning. What I was surprised about was the tone in his voice; he seemed a little nervous and embarrassed as he asked me if I would join him for lunch.

Earl was, at the time, an insurance executive and teacher of my Sunday School class at College Park Baptist Church in Greensboro, NC. He rose to the top of his profession by his Christian example, a testimonial not only to himself but also to those in his company who treasured and rewarded that trait. *Here* is a man who always spoke his faith, regardless of his surroundings, and was enabled to do so by his employer.

Tall, silver haired, always perfectly groomed and mannered, Earl's exterior was a window to his rock solid core of faith. One of my favorite stories involved his encounters in World War II, while serving as a Marine on Iwo Jima, with a certain non-believer. Every morning the Marine, who was an apparent exception to the theory about "foxhole" prayers, would tell Earl, "I didn't pray again last night, Reb." "Reb" being a nickname the man chose for Earl, for obvious reasons. The little sentence tells you how often Earl witnessed to the Marine: daily. By his constant vocal denials, the man unwittingly and unwilling passed on Earl's witness to the other Marines on a regular basis.

So God carried out His purpose through Earl, even in the face of denial. I don't recall that Earl ever was successful in helping the man, apparently a "Matthew 7:6 person,"64 to salvation, despite his efforts.

Earl's call to me on this day had something to do with the last will and testament of one of our sisters in Christ, who had just recently passed away. At the time, I had been an organizer of a group of men who cut grass for some of the ladies in the congregation, those who were elderly and widowed, single, or whose husbands were ill from serious disease. Earl's nervousness arose from the contents of the will, which he laid in front of me next to my salad. The sister had left money to the individuals in the group, by name….Dan, Jim, Bill…..every name except the organizer himself….me. We both realized that this wonderful lady, a former missionary, would never have done this intentionally.

As I looked at the will, my mind replayed my typical visit to the lady's home. Usually we worked in pairs. I would cut my half of the grass and usually, leave, right away. My partners would often stay and have some quality time with the sister, listening to her stories, sharing the gospel, whatever she needed to talk about, or whatever she could help them unburden from their own hearts.

By being so unimportant in filling her real need, the need of her heart rather than her lawn, I had been totally forgettable as a minister to her. Unintentionally, she probably perceived me as pasting that gold star on my book in heaven, an act of works without much faith. I hope that isn't entirely true, but I wasn't drawing a much better picture for her than that.

As I recall, although echoing Earl's feeling that the omission was unintentional, I was too embarrassed to tell him how I had acted. He explained to me that her executors had decided that I was entitled to my share of the money that she had willed to the group. I explained to Earl that I did not feel worthy of the money and that, as she had no heirs, I felt like the money should go to the church (I learned the others had also reached this same conclusion). It was agreed that this was how it was to be handled.

Postscript

Earl Ryals was the most Christlike manager I have ever known. Although I never had the pleasure of working directly with him professionally, our friendship allowed me to be the benefactor of many of his stories about management principles.

During one particular term of employment, I worked with many associates who had never, until then, been faced with the prospect of losing their jobs. As I fretted over how to comfort them in their first exposure to this danger, Earl shared with me this: convince them that they (and God) are "their own best security." In other words, teach them to develop themselves, not rely on any given employer to assure them of everlasting security. I used his lesson then, and have done so many times since, both with others and my own career plans.

I particularly enjoyed Earl's stories about his handling of recalcitrant or unmotivated subordinates. Without being the least bit confrontational, he would pay a visit to the unruly or idle associate, informing them that he had come to realize that the company was at fault for not blessing them with a rewarding workload, and then provide them with the additional blessing..

I was looking forward to sharing this story with Earl, who I hadn't spoken with in many years. His wife Inez was surprised to hear from me, since we had been separated by so much distance and time. After a few minutes of catching up on the usual issues: how were my kids, my church life, etc., she delivered the disappointing news. Earl was in the advanced stages of Alzheimer's. Inez explained that it would be best if I didn't try to stir what was left of his memory; he would not remember who I was. My heart sank, but of course I respected her request.

I know in my heart somehow that Inez, with God's help, will succeed in sharing this token of respect to a man I admire as much as any I have ever met. If not, I also know that I will share it with him personally someday in heaven. I was at least able to learn of Earl's conversion experience, which Inez shared without me even asking. During WWII, while on Maui, Hawai'i, Earl was baptized in a canal by a Marine chaplain.

THE OFFERING TAKERS

On the recurring theme of the inspiration of children, I have one last story to tell. It involves that part of the worship service where the plates are passed for the acceptance of the offering. My responsibility is the upper left-hand balcony (I call it the "not ready for prime time" spot). When I first "took the job," I found one of my Royal Ambassador kids,65 Josh, already on duty. While it was unusual for someone his age to be involved in this service, he obviously had been at it a long time, did a great job, and treated the process very reverently. In fact, I should most appropriately say he taught *me* the right way to do it.

One morning, a married couple and their children passed by me in my post and, for reasons I can't remember, mentioned how much their daughter Anna (age 10) loved this particular part of worship. Impulsiveness, for better or worse, is part of the wiring God bestowed on me. Without thinking too much about it, I offered Anna the opportunity to help on the following Sunday. On the appointed day, she showed up (as always) in a pretty dress, perfectly manicured, and she began to carry out her duties under my watchful eye. At this early stage, she was naturally a little nervous and required a bit of directing.

Now, as we all can anticipate, this aroused other kids' interest. I soon had four or five of them wanting to become part of the process. In the Sundays that followed, I incorporated a few of them (Javaris, Nick, Christopher, Caroline, Hannah, and Anna's even more diminutive cousin Bailie) into the service, with as much training as I could give them "on the fly" in the usual busy church schedule. The results were mixed. Some Sundays were pretty difficult, as everyone didn't always execute flawlessly (including me). I watched the eyes in the balcony, many smiled at the kid's efforts, but some looked less delighted with the idea. Anna seemed hardly bigger than the plates she was often required to carry. On one particular morning, one of the boys misunderstood my direction, I was not close enough to him to correct it, and plates went every which way. A visitor stood up in disgust and tried to conduct the process himself.

Frustrated, I asked Skip Balkcum, our chairmen of deacons, for his advice. I feared that the "experiment" might be having a counterproductive impact on the congregation. I knew that Skip had a similar dedication to involving kids in ministry; he had already led by example by involving a young man named Javaris (age ten) in the ushering process. Javaris, one of three children of one of our "single moms," helped us pass out church bulletins at the front foyer of the sanctuary.[66] Skip listened, made a few suggestions, and encouraged me to hang in there with the idea.

One morning, I went upstairs and the only reliable faces I could find were Josh's and Anna's. Apparently the adults who often helped were on vacation, so it was left to the three of us to cover the whole balcony. Josh took the left, Anna and I the right. I was apprehensive; Anna had not yet gotten thoroughly comfortable with things. And, to make matters worse, she wound up at the end of the last row, where she was required to stack the plates in her arms before moving to the upper rows of pews. She had never tried, much less mastered, that task. I imagined money flying everywhere. I watched as she gingerly assembled the plates and carefully stepped up to the upper level. I watched as she remembered the part where she had to hand me an extra plate, which she did without prompting. In the space of two minutes, she passed from nervousness to ushering perfection, right before my eyes. As we passed by her parents, I looked at them in pride and excitement and said, "She's doing this perfectly." When we were finished, I gave her a huge appreciative hug, which she barely understood; *she* knew she had done a good job, so what was the big deal?

In time, everyone grasped all the little nuances of the service, and now most Sundays go by uneventfully. But one thing will never change. Every Sunday, my heart is filled to the brim with the Holy Spirit as I watch those children go about a task that they revere and respect. I watch the eyes in the congregation shining as they watch the kids work (somehow, understandably, they shine a little brighter for the pretty girls like Anna and Bailey than they do for us guys!). It warms me in a unique way. I pray that the involvement is filling them with memories of responsibility that will make them want to stay in worship as they grow older, an important matter in these days when we lose so many as they enter adolescence.

Postscript

In the early stages of working with my young charges, I went to see the movie "Radio." The story involves a high school coach's dedication to a mentally challenged boy, and the obstacles he faces while working him into various roles supporting the football team. It is based on the true story of James Robert Kennedy and his mentor, South Carolina football coach Harold Jones. Kennedy's naive behavior leads to all manner of challenges for Jones: berating referees at inopportune times, causing a sea of yellow penalty flags; general discord among the barbershop "Monday Morning Quarterback" crowd, and so on. The coach never wavers from his support of the young man.

At various points in the movie, I admit I simply could not understand Jones' steadfast dedication to the young man in the face of the risks involved. Then I realized the movie was there to help me understand my commitment to the children. While my ushering challenges paled in comparison to the coach's, and my professional situation was certainly never endangered, I came to see the parallel. Just another case of God putting the right thing in front of me at the right time. Particularly since Margaret and I argued about which movie to see and almost went to something else! Like "Time Changer," the film helped me be a better Christian by displaying for me the proper attitude for the circumstance.

A final comment: the only time that money really "flew" during our offering service came as a result of one of my goofs. Hurrying, I wheeled around one morning to hand the plates to the people in the next set of pews. A folded check on top came out of the plate and helicoptered over the balcony rail, down toward the pews on the floor of the sanctuary. It landed squarely between two of my tenth grade boys, one of whom (Mike) picked it up, eyed it carefully, and laid it in the plate now passing by him, all without ever looking up to see where it came from.

REBA SIMS, DEN MOTHER

The nickname above comes from this fine lady's tireless support of the divorced-male dominated mission activities that originally brought me into contact with her67. To single out these particular activities is probably unfair; Reba is ever-reliable in *any* church activity to which she commits. And she commits to plenty. After watching her put heart and soul into whatever project is at hand, I have come to almost automatically wait for the signature comment "I'm sorry I didn't do as much with this as I should have."

It would be equally unfair to overemphasize Reba's most visible characteristic: her keen sense of accountability. Doing so might paint this gentle and kind woman as harsh and demanding, far from the truth. But, to be sure, any individual or church body that falls short of its appointed mission can count on meeting Reba's disappointment. One particular mental picture stands out; following a week spent trying to drum up support for a particular project. The picture: Reba, me, an empty fellowship hall, and six boxes of hot fresh donuts, a dozen to a box. I am still sure, from a backlit view, that the shimmering air around her head was truly steamed. Similar accountability is administered if support teams fail to have us in readiness for events such as the Single Mom's Oil Change, the Interfaith Hospitality program, and so forth.

Reba had been a vibrant part of Warren Baptist's ministries

for 33 years before I met her in 1999. In 1982, her husband Ray passed away. That sad event had the positive consequence of making her a beacon for Warren's singles program, and explains her prominence in the aforementioned projects.

Realizing that our short acquaintance meant that I was looking at a quality individual through my own small window, I asked Reba for a little history. What follows reemphasizes my belief that there are no "standard" paths to Christian service.

Reba, I learned, was not saved until the age of 30. Her own words of explanation are too poetic to rephrase, words neither rehearsed or postured, "For years and years, I wrestled with the thought that I would just never be good enough to be a Christian. Finally, I decided that this was true, I would indeed never be good enough, so I accepted salvation at the age of 30."

Born July 16, 1932, the 14th of 14 children, Reba's childhood was spent in the countryside, as of course was commonplace in those days. As a concession to the hard work of farming and the remoteness of her West Georgia homeplace, the church that she attended only met once a month. Her parents, Frank and Tessie Rogers, instilled in her a sense of honesty and reliability. They embodied the scriptural principles that speak to God's ownership of everything. They constantly shared with those less fortunate. In particular, Reba remembered their trips to into town; the basket of strawberries in the bed of the pickup truck for the family dentist, accompanied by other fruits and vegetables for everyone along the road between. Great pieces of Christmastime were spent sharing with those less fortunate. Frank and Tessie *never* spoke of their sacrifices. My small window widens so I can see the source of Reba's humility, walking up weathered doorsteps carrying nourishment for body and soul.

Following a personal dedication to be a benefit to others,

GOD SPOKE AND HE SOUNDED LIKE....

Reba studied medical technology, so that she would be able to help diagnose patient illnesses in the hospitals where she was employed. Her choice of career ultimately meant a move to "faraway Augusta." She was married to Ray Sims, seven years her senior, in August 1952. She had learned to quickly appreciate the maturity of Ray's manners and conduct. Frank, like most conservative fathers, was not yet quite so sure. Following the wedding, he told Ray "If you decide you don't like her, just bring her back to us." Ray would often say he was afraid to object to anything since Reba had a brother at each door of the wedding service to keep watch on him. Later, when the couple would return to visit family, Ray would say he had indeed brought Reba back but she wouldn't get out of the car.

They had two beautiful children, Linda and Ray, Jr. Following a long and happy marriage, Ray Sr. passed away in 1982 from the complications of diabetes.

Reba had reached a turning point in life; one which we almost all face at one time or another. At this time, she was a person of 50 years of age, who had already lived a productive life in one realm, the realm of married family and active employment. (At this point, Reba had also left the world of full time employment, at least in terms of the job market.)

By the late 1980's, the Lord had moved Reba into what would become years of meaningful service to the Warren Baptist singles program. Reba had become a member at Warren in 1965 but had never imagined this course, and in fact still could not quite think of herself as a single person. She was asked to accept the position of Director of the singles class at Warren, a large group of over 100. Although she confesses to having little idea how to direct, she prayed and threw her heart into the program, and God was there for her. She saw the importance of being on hand early on Sunday morning to make everyone feel welcome, a *very* important thing for singles to feel. She took classes at Ridgecrest Conference Center in Black Mountain, NC, and other venues. As she says, "I soaked up all the information I could so I could comfort those who I knew were hurting very badly, to bring them into the group." The seeds that Reba planted helped provide for a very vibrant and active singles ministry within Warren, a program that continues in the same fashion today.

The Scriptural View

As I poured over modern texts about women in the Bible, I came across a comment that God did not speak to men through women very often in Biblical times. In terms of the number of Biblical accounts, this is undeniably true but, just as clearly, that has changed.

Consideration of Reba's life cannot help but bring forth parallels to the lives of Naomi and her daughter Ruth, and the self-giving love these widowed ladies demonstrated. The book of Ruth is rich with the ministrations of a godly family demonstrating great faithfulness during hardship, as Reba and her parents likewise demonstrated. Naomi and her family suffered from famine similar to the hard times Reba's family suffered during the depression. Reba, like Ruth, "..left (her) father and mother and (her) homeland and came to live with a people (she) did not know" (Ruth 2:11 NIV). Reba, like Ruth, worked in the fields, fields which included populations of single, or single-again, men and women.

We can also look to the stories of Naomi, Abraham, and countless others in the Bible who saw age or other circumstance as the end of their usefulness in God's plans. As with Reba's life, how dramatically incorrect did these beliefs turn out to be?

We also find parallels in the lives of:
- Deborah, in the book of Judges, showing both her leadership and her support of an assembly of men: Barak and his army. In fact, Barak stated, "If you go with me, I will go, but if you don't go with me, I won't go" (Judges 4:8 NIV).
- Dorcas, in her selfless servanthood for her church as evidenced in Acts 9:36, where she worked to help the poor and needy. Reba's contributions to the Interfaith Homeless program often bore witness to her efforts in that direction.
- Lydia (Acts 16) supported men's ministries by providing shelter and support for Paul and his companions, as did Priscilla in Acts 18.
- Rebekah, the single woman who threw herself into selfless service in Genesis 24.

CONCLUSION

Preparing this material was a labor of love for me. My hope is that sharing this broad range of personal testimonials will help or inspire others in their daily walk. As Katie's mother said, if the sharing of these witnesses helps just one person (one person who becomes a more Christlike manager, one person who attacks a fear of public speaking, or is improved by any of the other issues addressed here), it will have been well worth it.

There are so many more stories which, unfortunately, could not be included here for reasons of space, timing, or context. There are so many more people to thank for their ongoing friendship, support and love. To Frankie Goodin, Jack Hook and Tim Jennings, my classmates in the Blended Family Sunday School Class, who held me accountable to finish this book. To Dr. David Fleming, who helped me move things along at a key point. To Greg Shuler, who so openly shared with me the scars from his own divorce. To Dave Walizer, for making me a part of his family at a crucial time in my life. To "the Jims" (Tomac and Collier), and Alan Smith, for their constant friendship, every day. To my brother Terry, for being my brother in every way. To my Royal Ambassador boys Braxton, Daniel, Grant, Jordan, Matthew, Nathan and Will for their inspiration and overwhelming love. A special thanks to Skip Balkcum for his marvelous counsel and encouragement in so many things I tackled. To Robert Hewett and Charles Lucas, who helped me with the facts on the stories about their fathers. To Inez Ryals, who did the same for the story on her husband Earl. To Kris Prior and Greg Harris, who were the "zip-drive" angels who rescued me from my deepest hour of technical despair. And, to the original people God spoke and He sounded like, Scott Torrence and Ron Howes.

And finally, to overcoming the devil, who drew up unimaginable obstacles to the completion of this manuscript. I am happy to tell him he lost the battle.

APPENDIX

A Christian's Hierarchy of Needs

Abraham Maslow, a groundbreaking psychologist who lived from 1908 to 1970, is most famous for introducing the theory of a human "Hierarchy of Needs." Maslow's observations of behavior in monkeys (!) led him to the realization that there is a tendency in living beings to take care of certain things first. For example, the tendency to satisfy physiological needs such as hunger, thirst, breath, and so forth before moving on to less pressing needs. Maslow ultimately categorized these needs into layers as shown below:

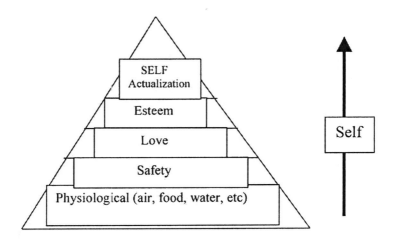

As I pondered the idea of translating Maslow's secular work based on monkeys into a Christian hierarchical model, I was first drawn to the word "SELF" at the top of his pyramid.68 The obvious first step in the translation process was to turn this level into its opposite form, *selflessness,* or "GOD centered."

Skipping the parts in between, I moved to the bottom, where of course we have *salvation*; nothing occurs without that. Then, logically we have *faith.* The next layers are open to individual interpretation; there are many choices, Biblical literacy being one. But, for the purpose of this model, what better coincidence than to, for once, emulate Maslow and use *love.* After all, without love, what execution of spiritual gifts is truly possible? Then, *works,* which I would offer cannot proceed properly without all of the other attributes.

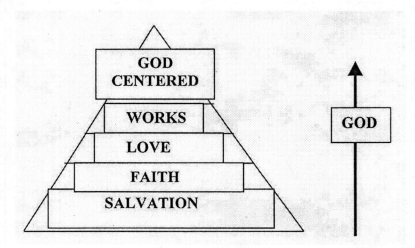

GOD SPOKE AND HE SOUNDED LIKE....

We wind up with a model that is obviously focused on growing more Godlike, as opposed to becoming more self serving.

BIBLIOGRAPHY

Bible History website www.bible-history.com

Biblical Illustrator, Volume 29, Number 3, Spring 2003, Lifeway Church Resources

Bowker, John, *God—A Brief History*, London, D K Publishing, 2002

Gallery, Jim, *Prayers of a Righteous Man,* Nashville, TN, Brighton Books

Hind, James F., *Business Leadership as Servant Leadership—Is Jesus a Useful Model to Follow?,* Cincinnati, Ohio, Forward Movement Publications, 1992

Journal of the Association of Christian Economists, No. 29, September 2001, Ceredigion, Wales, Great Britain

Kimbrough, Lawrence, *Words to Die For,* Nashville, TN, Broadman & Holman Publishers, 2002.

National Library of Australia, www.nla.gov.au

The World's Great Religions, NY, Time, 1957

ENDNOTES

[1] For those who will not believe, these struggles are their misguided "proof" of the Bible's "irreconcilable conflicts."

[2] To appreciate this, visit Jesus' words to the Roman Centurion in Matthew 8:6-13

[3] See Hebrews 11:13-16

[4] A friend of mine recently shared his belief that the term "lazy Christian" is an oxymoron.

[5] Maslow's highest "level," called "self-actualization, is often interpreted as "being all you can be." The spiritual parallel would be to become increasingly God centered. See Appendix

[6] I Kings 18

[7] In Luke 18: 13, "...the tax collector would not even look toward heaven, but beat his breasts and said 'God have mercy on me, a sinner.'" And Jesus said "...this man, rather than the other (the self righteous Pharisee) went home justified before God."

[8] I would blame the human business creation of the "corporation" for much of this. A corporation is, legally, a separate entity apart from those who operate it. Too often, this seems to offer escape from management accountability.

[9] His passionate claims that "reconciliation will do no good" simply support his more convenient attempts to sidestep the rules.

[10] Perhaps on a "lesser" note, things like widespread advertising of sexual stimulants on the radio and TV, or on the surface of products used in youth-attracting sporting events such as stock car racing.

[11] Thankfully, he returns home only AFTER he has gained the opportunity of sharing his heartfelt testimony with many of the characters in the movie, including Eddie, who he finally convinces to read the Bible. These accomplishments provide the most persuasive scenes in the film.

[12] In the process of writing this text, I even wrestled with how much easier it might be to make it a simple business book. Ultimately, I realized God sent me to "Time Changer" to teach me to avoid that thought. On the morning after I saw the film, I went to the gym to play a little basketball and write a chapter of the book; a chapter about one of the characters. Without knowing why, I wrote, instead, a "review" of Time Changer. I put it in the book as Chapter 20. It was a long time before I understood how really significant the chapter was.

[13] One Saturday every 90 days, we performed automobile lubrication services for any single mom in town who showed up. In five years (20 such events), God blessed us with clear weather on every occasion.

[14] See the chapter The Long Ten Feet, page 97.

[15] Accepting a minister's request that I teach this class taught me a lot about what spiritual gifts God had not blessed me with.

[16] By 52 A. D., Paul had journeyed as far west as Macedonia and Greece, creating powerful and influential churches along he way. By the year 380 A. D., Christianity was the official religion of the reunited Roman Empire.

[17] Time, NY 1957

[18] I had my own similar experience on Mt. Cotapaxi; see chapter on Ecuador

[19] Converted itself from public stock ownership to ownership by a small team composed of upper management and a venture capital group.

[20] Our challenges, however, paled considerably to those faced by an early missionary to the country, Jim Elliott. Jim eschewed domestic mission work, with the words "My going to Ecuador is God's counsel, as is my refusal to be counseled by all who insist I should stay and stir up the believers in the U. S. And how do I know it is His counsel? Yea my heart instructeth me in the night seasons." In January of 1956, he was murdered by local Auca Indians who misunderstood his motives.

[21] The "new" Center of the World is in a modern shopping plaza, where prices of local goods are, not surprisingly, much loftier than in the "old" center.

[22] The reason for this, I learned, often has to do with a country's taxation rules. A local showed me a house that had been contracted to be a two story dwelling. The first floor was complete and quite habitable. The second floor was, as mentioned above, nothing but randomly bent spikes of rebar. "When are they going to finish it?" I ignorantly asked. "Never," he replied. "If they do, they will have to pay taxes on it."

[23] Roses, one of Ecuador's top five exports to the U. S., were grown in this facility.

[24] The altitude was a challenge for all of us, as our youth learned the hard way attempting to play soccer with the local kids. Tiny natives ran circles around our gasping teens.

[25] The tallest member of our group was 6'3". The tops of the doorways struck him just above his eyebrows. Our smallest member, Wendell Duncan (see chapter Mary Duncan, Mother) dwarfed many of the natives.

[26] Marvelously effective and simple tools of witness available from EvangeCube International, Franklin, TN 888-354-9411,

www.evangecube.org. The company accepts testimonials by e-mail to testimony@evangecube.org.

[27] Quito was the location for the shooting of the movie "Proof of Life."

[28] One stop shopping is virtually unknown in Quito – one store for plywood, one for paint (pintura), one for hardware (tournillos = screws). "3 in 1" oil was obtained after I drew a series of pictures – the black oil drop drawn falling from the slender spout did the trick. I totally struck out looking for stain. Apparently there is no such product in Ecuador.

[29] The fascinating diary of William John Wills final days is available from the National Library of Australia website www.nla.gov.au/epubs.wills

[30] 70% of Ecuadorians live in poverty. Like El Salvador (see chapter Taxi Robert), the Ecuadorian economy was recently "dollarized." Missionary David Sills demonstrated to me the effect of this on the urban street vendors. Every merchant who offered his wares to our rolled-down car windows responded to the question "quanto" with the response "dollar." Regardless of the commodity sold, from beans to Spider Man outfits, the effect of the currency change has been to turn the Quito streets into a giant dollar store.

[31] Two interesting, but not surprising, sets of statistics speak to the medical and moral issues: infant mortality rate: U. S. 0.03%, Ecuador 0.68%; aids prevalence rate: U. S. 0.6%, Ecuador 0.3%.

[32] When he died, we were barely able to locate any of his family, finally finding a sister in New York who whisked away the body before we could arrange a local memorial service. "Joe's" only epitaph was the bottom half of a regatta announcement tacked to the bulletin board at the local yacht club; the poem "The Old Man and the Sea."

[33] As mentioned in he earlier footnote regarding corporations.

[34] Journal of the Association of Christian Economists, No. 29, September 2001

[35] In my business travels to Guatemala, I learned that the locals there have a term for unattached singles, "media naranja" which means half an orange, in search of the other half.

[36] A particularly exciting recent drive covered 150 miles in driving snow, unusual for our part of the world. A challenge my dad would have cherished, believing there was no snow condition in which he could not drive, well into his seventies, and being right about that.

[37] The property was finally taken over and turned into...... a large nightclub.

[38] And, to further convey the impact of this displacement, I should say that I have few if any relatives that I could even identify on sight, except my mother, father and brother.

[39] The closest similar experience for me occurred upon entering the Notre Dame de Bonsecours in a visit to Montreal, Canada. The few feet that separate the busy street from the hundreds of lit votives, the ornate painted carved wood, and the huge structure of blue stainglass cannot begin to prepare the visitor for what he or she will feel once inside.

[40] Billy is a refreshing individual. I will give away here a couple of his secrets. When asked by conservation minded visitors the source of the wildlife on exhibit, he routinely replies "road kill." He is very proud of his night time photography of local coyotes, badgers and other varmints, caught in the glare of his flashbulb. The fact that they look a lot like the stuffed animals on exhibit is not coincidental. Mail simply addressed "Billy Barron, Fort Mill, S.C." will reach him.

[41] Look at a map and find the areas around the towns of

Columbus, Clinton and Mayfield in Western Kentucky. Even today, you can see how isolated this area is from any major metropolitan area. We often swam in Reelfoot Lake, which had been formed by an earthquake in, of all places, New Madrid, Missouri, in the mid-1800's. The quake rang church bells in Boston, MA, the Mississippi ran backwards for an hour, and the overflow formed Reelfoot Lake.

[42] In the documentary "Roger and Me," the star is an endearing deputy sheriff named Fred whose job it is to evict people who have defaulted on mortgages or rent payments. (Those of us in the credit world can identify with how painful this has to be for Fred.) In one scene, he is about to evict a lady who has taken in a companion against Fred's earlier advice. He tells the camera "I told her several weeks ago that she didn't need any help being poor. She went out and got some help."

[43] Proverbs 18:16 says "A gift opens the way for the giver and ushers him into the presence of the great."

[44] One of the speakers at the seminar, a pilot, used the metaphor "potholes in the sky" for air turbulence. While not quite the same thing as making your whole speech metaphoric, it's an idea of how imagery can be used to spice up your talk.

[45] But, if your first few words are spoken with a bit of a shaky voice, drive on anyway, it happens and it's natural.

[46] A very thorough account of Barnabus appears in **Biblical Illustrator,** Volume 29 Number 3, Spring 2003.

[47] Where we first met when I moved to Charlotte from Dallas, Texas that year

[48] The area of Guatemala City where many American hotels operate; generally considered one of the safer areas for visitors. During my first trip, I learned the value of safety; six people were killed in various violent incidents. For example, a Japanese tourist was stoned to death, along with his Guatemalan bus

driver, by villagers who were disturbed by their picture taking and other actions. A prominent local newspaper photographer was also shot to death.

[49] To date, neither of us have had the chance to share this story, but God used the blank space to remind me of my own spiritual encounter in El Salvador. See "Taxi Robert – Speak English."

[50] This is a verse quoted by many in today's society, including single or divorced people struggling with finding lifetime partnership in the form of a mate.

[51] Eliminating its own local currency in favor of the dollar.

[52] Similar to NAFTA; made certain exports of Latin American products to the U. S. "duty free."

[53] Where state divorce laws permit such choices.

[54] "Real integration" did not occur until Robert entered the 11th grade, when "busing" brought him back into academic fellowship with many of his elementary school companions.

[55] Not a hard love to understand; Henry Ford, reflecting on how little pleasure his material wealth had brought him, once commented he had been happier as a mechanic.

[56] Whose last name, ironically, was "Hazzard."

[57] Another precious moment came when, as a member of the choir of my predominately white church, I helped sing the "Share the Light" cantata in a special Sunday Night service at this same predominately black church.

[58] A day set aside to encourage race relations, sponsored by the Southern Baptist Convention

[59] A similar experience for me involved a local rabbi who was invited to our protestant church to share Jewish culture; including breaking of bread for Passover. Many people were

very challenged by this activity, both in our congregation and his.

[60] In this situation, "dressing down" the offending salesman would have been unwise. Learning a lesson "on the fly," I simply explained to the staff that they were clearly being manipulated and would have been better advised to have declined the offer

[61] The scholarship continues to this day, and many worthy young credit professionals have benefited from the ongoing funding provided by the professional association.

[62] April 2004, Buena Vista Magazines

[63] In the original e-mail, the real names of the school, city and church were divulged. Vinny and I were both concerned that the young lady had, in these frightening times, revealed too much and deleted these details from the copies we distributed to others, and likewise are they omitted here.

[64] Matthew 7:6 speaks to those individuals who simply refuse to accept salvation regardless of the level of godliness of the witnesses put in their path (they trample the sacred under their feet). This parallel was the subject of a sermon from Dr, Frank Page of First Baptist Church of Taylors, SC.

[65] A Baptist children's program for boys in grades 1 through 6. I serve as a counselor for the 4th grade.

[66] One Sunday morning, after we ran out of bulletins, Javaris suggested (with a twinkle in his eye) that we pass out the Senior Times. He really didn't need me to explain why this would not be a universally good idea.

[67] For example, the Hammer 'n Nails home repair program and the Single Mom's Oil Changes.

[68] Refer to the end of the chapter Stones for some additional insights on the concept of monkeys and value systems.

Made in the USA